M000196315

HOW TO DRINK LIKE A MAD MAN

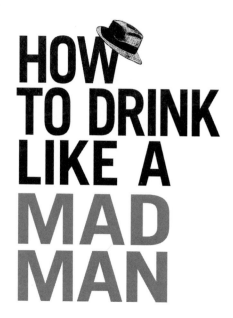

HOW TO DRINK LIKE A MAD MAN

RALPH MALONEY

Illustrated by Leo Summers

DOVER PUBLICATIONS, INC., Mineola, New York

Photographs courtesy of ThinkStock.com. Copyright © 2012

Bibliographical Note

This Dover edition, first published in 2012, is an unabridged, newly reset republication of *The 24 Hour Drink Book: A Guide to Executive Survival*, originally published in 1962 by Productions 14, New York. A new selection of photographs has been specially added to this edition.

Library of Congress Cataloging-in-Publication Data

Maloney, Ralph.
    How to drink like a mad man / Ralph Maloney ; illustrated by Leo Summers.
      p. cm.
    Originally published: The 24 Hour Drink Book: A Guide to Executive Survival. New York: Productions 14, © 1962.
    ISBN-13: 978-0-486-48352-8
    ISBN-10: 0-486-48352-5

HV5275 .M2 2012
362.292—dc23

2011031225

Manufactured in the United States by Courier Corporation
48352501
www.doverpublications.com

CONTENTS

FOREWORD

AN AUTHORITATIVE STATEMENT

concerning why this book was written
what it can and cannot possibly
do for you and why it is a suitable
volume for business giving

THE SUBJECT of this slender but ambitious volume is another of the successes of American Business Life, the successful drinker.

We shall refer to him as the Working Lush in order to avoid the usual boozy connotations of the term *drunk*. Our man has never seen the Bowery—and never will. He knows only by hearsay that the Third Avenue El is down, or that the West Side is there at all. He is respected in his work and home community; he makes a lot of money; he looks better in the morning than many of the younger, soberer men around him; and he is a little drunk always.

How does he do it? How, for that matter, could you do it? This book is an inspection of the attitudes, techniques, and devices the successful drinker uses to keep the world at bay and his fortunes flourishing.

We shall attempt here to provide certain of the methods. But be advised: This tract is more than a list of useful *dos* and *don'ts*. It is a guide to the richer enjoyment of the drinking life. Use it as such.

There are, first, Two Rules that you must carry in your consciousness always.

Rule One is simply this: *Realize that you are a Working Lush*. This does *not* mean that you are sick. Neither is it a preface to any decision to abandon alcohol. It is a simple statement of fact. Once this difficult bit of self-knowledge has been digested, you are on your way to success in modern business life.

Rule Two: *Drink one day at a time, one drink at a time.* Commit this rule to memory—or better, your memory being what it is, write it down on the back of your wife's picture where no one will ever look, and carry it in your wallet.

Having defined the twin rocks upon which Success is built, let us proceed to some techniques.

THESAURUS

NOMENCLATURE AND SEMANTICS play so large a part in the success pattern of the Working Lush that it is imperative they be dealt with at the inception of this treatise.

The first thing you must do is cleanse your mind of all the comfortable and familiar terms common to The Art: *saloon, mart, lush, belt, double,* and a host of others. These words are replaced by circumlocutions, gaucheries, and outright misnomers. Examples follow.

For the Drink, or Fix

For anybody but the real Veteran, it is okay to use the word *drink* in offering or accepting a Fix. But it is a borderline word, best shunned by those who have given themselves over entirely to alcohol. Working Lush, greeting a guest, says, "Come on in, Roland. How about a highball or a cocktail?" These are terribly gauche words, not heard in any decent saloon since World

War Two (when saloons teemed with amateur drunks). They will establish you at once as a sober-sides.

A glass of whisky can be a marvelously misleading phrase if whisky comes out like a sneeze. One example of its use appears later, under "A BAR IN THE OFFICE." Yet the phrase is better used in discussing whisky's mythical restorative powers. As, on a week-end at the Board Chairman's country retreat, W.L. returns from a long hike in the cold. (He has been looking for a Roadhouse.) Stamping his feet on the kitchen floor, he rubs his hands briskly together and says, "Man! I could use a glass of whisky." Thus he gets his morning Fix while all hands consider him a ruddy outdoorsman.

There are other words that can be adapted to this purpose. *Aperitif,* for example, or *digestive.* Consider *liqueur.* "I think I might have a small liqueur," replaces the harsh, "Dry stinger, rocks," and properly manipulated will get you the same thing.

Also drop the comradely specifics used to describe containers of booze. *Pint, fifth, quart, split, half-gallon,* and *jug* are all dropped from the vocabulary, to be replaced by the wonderfully naive "a bottle of whisky." When told you are holding a fifth of gin, not a bottle of whisky, shrug and smile, saying, "It's all too much for me, anyway." The response will send a real thrill through the cockles of your cunning.

For the Saloon, or Bar

A saloon is any place that sells liquor for consumption on the premises. Others may be deceived by elaborate decor and magnificent cuisine, but not the lush. To him, a saloon is a saloon.

While this gives him a certain clarity of vision in judging "21" or the Chambord, it reflects a definite prejudice. He never refers to these landmarks as "swell saloons." He cuts the word *saloon* from his vocabulary altogether. This creates the problem of finding smokescreen words to replace it.

(W.L., in a wistful slip, said once of the cafeteria at the Central Park Zoo, "A swell saloon. Trees and seals and everything...." Fortunately, he was overheard only by his daughter, a nine-year-old stranger who could make no use of what she had learned.)

Far and away the best thing to call a saloon is a *Store*. Everybody in the whisky business calls saloons Stores. Thus you imply a solely commercial relationship between yourself and the beloved premises. Any subsequent demonstration of saloon lore on your part will be explained away by others, because you "...apparently were in the liquor business at one time, National Distillers or something."

Store, unfortunately, is of limited use. You can hardly say to the Chairman of the Board, "Let's have lunch at this terrific *store* I know." So you call the saloon a German (or French, or Italian) restaurant. Or, again, turn to the hotels in your neighborhood. Who can cavil at, "How about lunch at the Sheraton?" You say it in a kind of off-hand manner, secure in the knowledge that there are two fine saloons in the Sheraton.

For evening drinking, or Finishing Off, there are two names of such gaucherie that at first you will have trouble uttering them. These are *night club* and *cocktail lounge*. (Practice getting them out without giggling.) When you find yourself hung-up on the road with the Sales Manager, that practice will pay off. To him, *night club* means entertainment and music, *cocktail lounge* means girls and sex. To you, of course, they are two different kinds of saloon. With any luck, the Sales Manager will chase girls all night long (striking out from both sides of the plate), while you Finish Off on the old expense account.

The Great Bock Dodge

When you need a Fix, you need alcohol. This doesn't have to be gin-on-the-rocks or bourbon neat. As long as there's alcohol in it, a Fix is a Fix. For variety's sake, let's suppose our Working Lush is an outside man temporarily prevented from Nipping In through the presence of a Big Account. This is what he does:

W.L.: I'm thirsty, for some reason. Mind if we stop for a Coke?

B.A.: Not at all. I could use a Coke myself.

W.L.: Hey, how about that! The Bock (or May Wine) sign is in the window of that German restaurant (*sic*). Let's try it. I don't know when I had real Bock last.

The Bock Dodge is seasonal. Bock and May Wine apply in the spring. If a similar emergency arises in the dead of winter, say you are freezing to death and could use a hot chocolate. Then discover a Hot Toddy or Tom & Jerry sign and lead the Big Account to the saloon so decorated. In summer's heat, announce that you are dying for an "ice-cold glass of beer." Plead the bourgeois myth that "only beer can really quench that thirst."

The phrase *Irish Restaurant* is a contradiction in terms capable of provoking considerable mirth. One day some scholar, or team of scholars, will discover a proper name for the Irish Saloon, so that the Working Lush can, in decency, walk through that door in the morning. Be sure the name will be found, for Irish saloonkeepers have a gimmick for the respectable ingestion of alcohol at all hours called Irish Coffee. It is a beautiful Fix. Generations to come will evolve some circumlocution to make Irish Coffee available at 11:20.

For Fellow W.L.'s

In referring to (*i.e.*, squealing on) fellow Working Lushes, Aspiring Young Drunks, Impoverished Amateurs, and Outright Alcoholics, do *not* identify them by their true class. Dip into the wealth of archaisms supplied by the enduring love of booze among English-speaking peoples. *Drunkard* is a handsome word, its effectiveness augmented by overtones of assailing Puritanism. *Tosspot* has a gay ring to it, and should only be used in squealing on Lushes whom you rather like. *Barfly* sounds sordid. It may give a surly co-worker exactly what he has coming to him. *Tank* has a gargantuan feel and really won't do much harm, so use *Souse* to describe a man you'd just as soon have out of the way.

Certain phrases, spoken in awe but without a leer, can devastate a competitor. "I don't know where he puts it all," and "…Max had all of us under the table," will inflict immense damage on a Career. Best of all, single out a competitor who quite clearly should have Called In and say, "Charlie, I don't know how you do it. You look like a million dollars. You must have the stamina of a horse!" And everybody looks at Charlie, who is helpless, and Charlie is out of the way.

And, Inversely . . .

The subconscious will have its revenge for what is suppressed. The words you have cut from your vocabulary will leap to your lips in critical situations or when you have rendered yourself defenseless.

Let them leap. Let them nourish and enrich your speech. Suppose that you are sniping during the morning meeting and the word *lush* springs to mind. Use it. A *lush* opportunity, or meadow, or girl, you might say, gaining a minor reputation as an orator.

In these terms, *mart* becomes poesy for marketplace or forum. Better yet, *belt* can be used as, "a *belt* in the kisser," which is not only archaic and gauche, but is man-talk. *Fifth* thus becomes a movement in a "well-orchestrated sales symphony" or the Avenue delineating your westernmost foray.

Best of all is *shot*. When your subconscious thrusts this word to your lips (saying to you, perhaps, "God, how you need a *shot*!"), seize the word and use it. It is an okay word, like *Sun* and *Gym, Theater* or *Restaurant.* Kids and puppies and wives get all kinds of *shots* nowadays. As, "What this program needs is a couple of shots…! to get it off the ground." Or, discussing a company film, the word *shot* leaps to your quavering lips as you say, "I think the best way to open this thing is with a *shot*...." Don't stammer or flush. Conclude calmly, "...of our Hartford plant, showing all the chimneys." (But don't start clapping or laughing. To all but the Fellow Lushes in your audience, what you have said is not clever, only safe.)

Chapter One

THE HOME

SUCCESS HAS ITS PRICE. The Working Lush, like other artists, is a lonely man. The isolation is the more painful for W.L. because, *un*like other artists, he is seldom alone. His problem is that in the crowds around him there is nobody in whom he can confide, no one he can trust. (Least trustworthy of all are his fellow Working Lushes, for, if they are successful men, be sure they are cunning and without loyalty of any kind.)

The isolation begins in the morning, in the home. W.L. awakes alone and muddled. His craft deprives him of the most primitive of solace, that knowledge of personal history called *memory*. (It will be noon or later before he can recall what he did the Night Before.) This is not entirely a debit. What he did the Night Before was probably embarrassing

and best forgotten. Thus, W.L. taps some sustenance from his very bewilderment. He says to himself (and only to himself, *no one* being trusted with this information), "I'm a Lush." So saying, he goes forth to pursue his Art afresh. In the ordinary run of circumstances, his first contact is with his wife.

W.L. and His Wife

Working Lush examines his wife swiftly before saying so much as good morning. Prolonged scrutiny is rude and lends an ox-like quality to the hungover man, so W.L. looks quickly for two things: (1) Is she talking? (2) Is she talking only to the children? If the answers are in sequence, "No" and "Yes," he makes a comment bespeaking absolute personal organization, as: "Conway has asked me to test-fire his new rifle at Abercrombie & Fitch at three-twenty-five this afternoon."

If the reply is, "I hope you blow your head off," then W.L. knows that whatever it was he did the Night Before, it has provoked no more than ordinary rancor. If, however, she turns on him, snarling, to say, "There is no Conway. He is a fiction you have created to explain torn garments, bruised flesh, and prolonged absences from home," then W.L. knows he was Pretty Bad last night. That memory will serve up, all morning, short takes of monstrous idiocy, starring himself.

In any event, W.L. avoids a clash with his wife the first thing in the morning. It is a lousy way to start the day, and he doesn't have a chance in the world of winning *any* argument. He has no idea what he did or said six hours earlier and cannot defend himself.

A final word regarding his wife. W.L. reflects from time to time on the hapless life his wife is leading—interpreting his mumbling, apologizing to practically everybody sooner or later, undressing him, etc.—and he has spells of compelling fondness, inspired by her profound loyalty to him. He also contemplates, with a glow like love, the strength there must be in that small body to carry him off to bed on occasion. When he thinks of these things, W.L. has a desire to unburden himself, to speak the magic sentence aloud: "I am an alcoholic."

He does not. For she will nod, and smile, and file that sentence away, and bludgeon him absolutely to death with it on an occasion of her choosing—Christmas Eve, perhaps, or the day following the Company Picnic. W.L. keeps his counsel. Lushing is a solitary craft, but it has its rewards.

W.L. and His Children

Conceived in stupor, W.L.'s children are high-strung, lacking in vigor, noisy and assertive. W.L. sees little of them because they are asleep when he gets home at night. When they get old enough to stay up later, they are Sent Away to School.

But while the children are too young to Send Away (or if Daddy has been spending all his money on Sauce and cannot afford School), the presence of children can be turned to advantage. Having children around in the morning, for example, is generally a *plus*. W.L. is desperately nice to his children in the short time he must abide them, and with good reason.

Only a child—and a youngish child, at that—can be unaware that the man he is talking with (His Father) is in the very lists of dissolution. Only a child will converse with a recently awakened Working Lush and not inquire how he plans to stay alive until 11:20 (an hour that takes on meaning later in our discussion). The Drinking Daddy, therefore, has an innocent audience before which to *practice talking*—to work the quaver from his voice, and on very bad mornings, to Remember Language. And, further, to recall by whom he is employed and for what purpose. If he promises them a lot of things (next week, next summer) the children will listen uncritically. This lends W.L. some of the confidence he will need to issue commands to adults later in the morning.

Grooming

Of utmost importance to W.L. is his grooming. This begins with The Bath.

Although he has spent much of his adult life making jokes about water (it rusts pipes, people drown in it, fish make love in it), W.L. inwardly respects water because *it works*: it does everything that is asked of it, and in his case much more. He adjusts the shower to achieve a maximum volume of water at a moderate temperature and utterly inundates himself for five minutes, soaping and rinsing several times. The water in W.L.'s shower remains at precisely the temperature first established. Nobody in his family big enough to reach a faucet would dare to turn it on while Daddy is in the shower.

W.L. keeps his hair close-cropped at all times, so it will not cascade over his eyes during a Prolonged Bout. Thus he can thrust his head into the stream of the shower, enjoy its enormous restorative effect, and not look like a Rube the rest of the day.

The successful Working Lush is clean-shaven. A moustache or beard is a mark of vanity, and he doesn't have time to be vain. Also, he is clean-shaven because later in the day, when he may be altogether in The Bag, facial hair makes a sloven of him. Back when he was a young Journeyman Drunk, W.L. adopted the electric razor because it is safer to operate with a pronounced tremor. (Although, to be perfectly fair, one morning W.L.'s hand shot up and removed much of his right eyebrow. This gave him a look of perpetual inquiry, so that for days people asked him what he wanted, when precisely what he wanted most was to be left alone. Still, it was infinitely easier to endure and explain than recurrent and unstanchable flesh wounds around the collar.)

W.L.'s teeth are meticulously cared for, briskly scrubbed each morning, and cleaned every month by his dentist. The neglected (or blue) tooth is the badge of the Impoverished Amateur. No need to ask, "With all his lushing around, where does he find time for the dentist?" He is a professional. Later, under "NOT GOING TO LUNCH," we will see how and why he *makes* time.

The Wardrobe

Here we speak of the hard-finished fabric and the dull hue. W.L. shuns tweeds because when he gets lumpy in a saloon tweeds make him look lumpier. His trousers are crisply pressed always, so that he will seem quite upright when, indeed, his knees are buckling. He sends his suits to the cleaners with scrupulous regularity; as a career drunkard, he is frequently spilled- or slobbered- upon by his inferiors. The elbows of his coats are inspected regularly for puddle-rings. When the elbows have been buffed shiny by bars, the suit is retired. W.L. purchases suits of dark blue worsted so that cigarette holes in the trousers can be camouflaged by swabbing the underlying fabric with blue-black ink.

In choice of neckwear, there is no dogma. On the one hand, the four-in-hand tie can be said to convey maturity and stability. Yet the bow tie lends the wearer a brisk, even boyish, air. Bow-tie adherents point out that the four-in-hand can be tugged down during Serious Drinking, resulting in a bum-like dishevelment. Still, the bow tie can work its way under the ear on occasion, making one look the idiot. It's a toss-up, really.

There is, however, no controversy in the matter of the shirt. It must be white. Absolutely white. Not eggshell, or off-white, and above all not blue. Even the most expensive blue shirt becomes working-stiff denim on a lush.

Chapter Two

OFF TO THE OFFICE

Our hero is now dressed. Murine in his eyes, mint on his breath, a stiff dose of astringent slapped manfully on his cheek, he is ready to go to The Office.

W.L. is a commuter. Thus, he enjoys a distinct advantage over those Working Lushes who do not commute: he has plenty of time to *practice talking* on the train. He can continue to work the quaver out of his voice by chatting with fellow commuters who are far below him in the corporate hierarchy. (Note: Non-commuting lushes are advised to buy a dog and walk it every morning. The exercise is not harmful, and they will encounter other dog-owners with whom to discuss worms, conjunctivitis, inbreeding, and soiled rugs. All this is admittedly dull, but the content of the talk does not matter. It is talk—a chance to *practice*.)

A sample train conversation follows:

W.L.: (after clearing his throat of rasp) Good morning, Patsy. Fine sunburn you have.

Patsy: It is flush, not sunburn, W.L. With any luck, I'll be dead by noon.

W.L.: (here he practices sounding *concerned*) Ah. Nothing wrong at home is there?

Patsy: Oh, nossir. But I just may have the hangover of my generation.

W.L.: (here he practices *laughing*. Just a light laugh, not enough to precipitate the coughing fit) Tied one on, did you, Son? Must have been some Occasion. (See "THESAURUS.")

Patsy: Yes. It was Tuesday!

(he laughs, has coughing fit, recovers, and stares through streaming tears at countryside, swallowing for all he is worth.)

Thus W.L. organizes his voice and demeanor on the trip to the city, practicing the various attitudes (affability, authority, concern, solicitude, censure) he will be expected to personify at The Office (while at heart feeling none of them, feeling, in fact, only hungover).

A few final words on commuting: Stay out of the smoking car. Not only do cigarettes make you shake, but their fragility is such that they become a prime means of advertising a tremor. Secondly, *stay awake* on the train. If you doze off for only a minute or two, your voice will congeal, your eyes will blear, and the healing work of the morning will have been wasted.

Calling In

There are mornings when no amount of medication or grooming will repair the ravages of the Night Before. On such mornings, do not under any circumstances go to the office until you are Restored. Call In.

Once a year, W.L. calls the president of his firm and says, "I have a hangover and I am staying in bed." This creates the illusion that he is forthright, something every bit as indispensable to him as the bottle in his desk. Note that he does not call his secretary, no matter what his excuse. That is not Playing the Game. Worse, it is suspect. W.L. always talks directly to The Old Man. (Fortunately, T.O.M. is indulgent of an occasional "youthful escapade"—his own occasional escapades being aimed as nearly in that direction as his age will permit.)

W.L. long ago acquired a useful disease. Malaria is a fine disease, but the Chairman of the Board was already using malaria, so W.L. acquired enteric. Enteric is the best disease of all for a lush to acquire because it recurs frequently and the attacks include such handy symptoms as sweats, shakes, and loose bowels. In addition, whenever it becomes necessary for W.L. to go away for a spell to Dry Out, he tells everybody it's the Old Enteric again, and nobody can challenge him.

It is by no means necessary to Call In from home and stay home on mornings when you can't quite get Restored. That's done only in desperation. Call instead from Grand Central and say your "breakfast meeting" is just getting underway. Allow an hour to try drinking a little coffee, then call The Office again to say you will be in the United Nations Delegates' Lounge or some other logical or euphonious place where you cannot be reached by telephone. First thing you know, it is 11:20 again and everything is fine.

Calling In Sick

If he cannot possibly leave his bed for the day, W.L. does not sleep late and then Call In. He calls promptly at nine, *then* goes back to sleep until two. He tells The Office he'll call again after the doctor leaves, thus guarding against interruption and seizing the initiative as his own.

Whenever possible, W.L. does not use illness as his excuse when Calling In. He lets it be known, for example, that he is active—perhaps a leader—in his community. "The Town Council is voting on wooden groins for the beach today. I figure to be pretty late." Somebody, one day long ago, convinced Management that it is to their advantage to have their employees active in whistle-stop community activities. Don't fight it.

Above all, do not have your wife call in for you. Despite the fat stake she has in your continued corporate legerdemain, her morning rancor certainly will cause her to botch things up, as, "W.L. can't make it in today. He drank a bad cold."

If there is a morning meeting that *must* be attended, and he is still far from Restored, W.L. uses certain tranquilizers and stimulants to sustain him until 11:20. These drugs are discussed elsewhere in this Guide. (See "CHEATING.")

The Last Mile

The temptation to tarry between station and office (and perhaps to accelerate the healing process with a nourishing Nip) is nigh overpowering. The successful Working Lush resists it manfully. Crew-cut head erect, crisply creased trousers lending authority to his step, he strides to his office.

At The Office he is presented with a second temptation: to practice talking to the receptionist or to his secretary. But while they may both be quite stupid, these young things sense more than they can possibly know. They may hunch that there is something wrong with a grown man who wants to chat with them the first thing in the morning. Out of their confusion, when W.L.'s back is turned, they may giggle. Abruptly, his confidence is so much smoke. No, he says only "Good morning" to these young ladies. He says it genially and without warmth, indicating preoccupation, and strides to the shelter of his office.

The brief business day is begun.

Chapter Three

OFFICE PROCEDURE

THE SUCCESSFUL WORKING LUSH keeps his office door open at all times. To shut it is to hide. Hide only in extreme emergencies: those mornings when you realize all too late that you should have Called In. When such an emergency arises, tell your secretary you are not to be disturbed, then behind the closed door, talk loudly and endlessly into your dictating machine. This procedure is called "closeting yourself to get some work done." Actually, it is not necessary to speak coherently into the machine, or in fact to pay any attention at all to what you are saying. (Extravagant encomiums to yourself are pleasant. Childhood rhymes are not recommended: they elude the memory over the years and can prove annoying.) After you can safely open the door again, make a business of stuffing the recorded tapes into

your brief case. No one will think to ask why you are doing this, in particular your secretary, who has been dreading all morning the endless transcription she is facing.

The Walking Wounded

Statistics show that between 4 per cent and 6 per cent of the employees of any large corporation are lushes of one kind or another. (These statistics were compiled by Yale University, clearly no place to send a child.) As the most pedestrian amateur drunk knows, no less than 60 per cent of every office staff are Sometime Drunks. This is both an advantage and a disadvantage.

On the one hand, the growing incidence of alcoholism among white-collar workers has assured that there are fewer meetings before 11:20 than there used to be. On the other, hungover co-workers now seek to establish a community of pain with the hangovers around them. Frequently you may be tempted to swap stories and sympathies with a cohort who confides, grimacing, that he is in very bad shape.

W.L. disciplines himself. He remembers that his is a lonely craft. Faced with the distressful figure of a Journeyman, deserving only contempt, he handles it thus:

Journeyman: W.L., you look as bad as I feel.

W.L.: (ruefully) Must be the Old Enteric kicking up again, Lloyd. What's your trouble?

Journeyman: This time I did it. Really did. I went the route this time, all right.

W.L.: (aloof, with mild distaste) Hangover?

Journeyman: (grunts and mutterings, signifying assent).

W.L.:	(paternal, yet faintly ominous) Take it easy on that stuff, young fella. I've seen more than one man drink himself out of a good job.
Journeyman:	(aware that he has delivered himself to the enemy) I don't usually have any…it was my wife's birthday, you see, and we…(he falters, quits, numb and cuffing imaginary lock from his forehead.)
W.L.:	(dismissing him) Well, I've got a lot of work to do. Want to drop over to the gym at lunch for a workout?
Journeyman:	No, I….
W.L.:	My best to your wife.
Journeyman:	My wife?

W.L.:	On her birthday.
Journeyman:	(routed, leaving) Oh, yes. Well, haha. Happy birthday.

This is cruel, perhaps, but it must be done. Lushes are a cunning and deceitful lot. Not a one of them is to be trusted. Had W.L. not dismissed the Journeyman so energetically, this very scene might well have taken place between the Journeyman and the Chairman of the Board, later in the day:

C.B.:	You're not looking very well, son.
Journeyman:	I might have picked up some of W.L.'s enteric. (leers.)
C.B.:	(whose fraudulent malaria got him where he is today) Terrible thing, that enteric.

Journeyman:	Must be. Makes W.L. shake like he'd been on a three-day bat.
C.B.:	Our Group Health may cover it. I'll check on that with Accounting, for you and W.L. Ah, I remember how the Insurance Boys came through for me after that last malaria bout....

Thus, a soft answer turneth away the Journeyman's wrath. Nevertheless, seeds of suspicion have been sown in Management Minds. Years of patient deceit have been brought to naught. No, W.L. is not cruel in dealing with hungover amateurs and journeymen. He is only doing what is necessary for the protection of himself and the preservation of his Art.

The Telephone

The Working-Lush-Executive's telephone is a pronouncedly schizoid instrument. In the morning it is a shrill tyrant; in the afternoon it is a boon companion and a swell way to kill time. Master the telephone in its two personalities.

No matter how much you practice on the train, your voice is unsteady in the morning. Hold the telephone four good inches from your mouth and shout at it. No quaver will betray you and everybody on the floor will know you are in and At Work. In the afternoon, there is a tendency to be garrulous and quite loud. Suppress this tendency rudely and you will sound the same on the telephone in the afternoon as you sound in the morning.

There is a female disorder which strikes the alcoholic in the afternoon. Known as "telephonitis," it is symptomized by a desire to call everybody you have ever known and an absolute passion to call the Coast or the Vatican. Here again discipline is the answer. *Don't pick up that phone unless it rings.*

After three, your diction is impaired. Sit up very straight, hold the instrument at an awkward angle, make yourself as uncomfortable as possible in every way. Research reveals no more than a "post hoc" relationship between diction and discomfort, but the connection is there, nonetheless. Ecclesiastical history supports it. For centuries, monks improved their diction in prayer by kneeling on cold, unyielding surfaces. W.L. used to kneel on the floor while talking on the phone until promotions put a deep pile rug in his office. Now he jams the fingers of his free hand in the top drawer of his desk.

The Water Cooler

Somewhere in every office there is a device to supply drinking water to the employees. The lush has, on any given morning, an ungovernable thirst. Never slake this thirst at the water cooler. If it is at all possible, don't go near the water cooler at all. Folk wisdom has it that a man with a hangover is terribly thirsty. Folk wisdom is absolutely right. By making repeated trips to the source of water, you are announcing that you have a hangover and people will start making jokes about you.

What to do? You have an ungovernable thirst and the water cooler is off-limits.

Get a plant. Get several plants and put them on a shelf in your office. Beneath the shelf install a gallon jug of water. Smear the jug with mud so the connection between it and the plants is manifest. Pour frequently into an unromantic tumbler sort of glass on your desk. Don't, in God's name, belt from the jug. If you are seen, nothing you can say in explanation can rescue you. You will have become a figure of censure and fun.

In the extreme cases when your water jug is empty and you have already made one trip to the water cooler—yet thirst persists—do *not* go to the men's room and drink from the tap. The men's room is crowded mornings. How are you to know who may be sitting in a booth while you're guzzling from a sink? Yet all is not lost. In an untraveled corner of every floor of every large building, there is a small room with an enormous sink called the "broom closet," or "mop room," or "Porter's room," or some such. It is terribly small and out-of-the-way, or the landlord would rent it. Slip into the closet, thrust your head under the tap and drink yourself back into shape.

Coffeetime

The coffee break kills time. It picks up the slack in the middle of the morning. Thus it is popular with lushes and abstainers alike because it is something to *do*. While you are as eager as the next chap to eat up the empty hours of morning, there are a few precautions that you, as a lush, must take before killing time over coffee.

1. Do not quench your thirst on coffee. It is a stimulant and destructive of poise. Drink lots of water, then nurse the coffee.

2. Even as a democratic gesture, never go to the coffee cart yourself. Send a girl, any girl. Those containers are scalding hot, uninsulated, and are filled to the brim by that spy from Schrafft's. One morning your tremor will go absolutely wild in a terribly public circumstance.

3. Establish that you have a favorite cup, or mug. Never drink coffee from the carton. The paper container that will hold hot coffee and withstand a bad case of shakes has not yet been devised. Before your panicked eye, right in your trembling, scalded hand, that carton will peel apart at the seams like a hollyhock at morning. And there you are, you and your blotter covered with coffee, at 10:15 A.M.

Chapter Four

AS YOU LAY DYING

WITH ANY KIND OF JOB AT ALL, you need not arrive at the office before 9:20. That means there are two long hours to live through until it is 11:20. In their awful way, these one-hundred-and-twenty minutes winnow the professional from the amateur, the Lush from the Sometime Drunk. For it is now that the hungover man is most vulnerable, the Citizen most formidable.

It frequently seems, in this period, that you are weapon-less. You cannot think; you can talk only with difficulty; you lack the co-ordination needed to manipulate small objects.

But you are not without a prized weapon.

As the other senses become sharper when one sense is impaired, so the Lush's cunning is honed by hangover,

debilitude, and all-round helplessness. Discussed below are certain devices, some *dos* and several *don'ts*, guaranteed to see you through the most agonizing morning.

Cheating

First, however, let's take a look at the various medicines— emergency measures only—which can be used on those mornings when even W.L.'s cunning is impaired. (When, certainly, he should have Called In.)

At the top of the list are tranquilizers. Now everybody knows any tranquilizer will cool you off sufficiently to beard the Chairman at his Board. But the side effects, hushed up by the Drug Cartel, are insidious. Worst of all, you neither need nor want a Fix at 11:20; you don't care. Then you don't feel much like a martini before lunch. And it gets worse: you don't feel much like a drink at 5:30, so you order a washy beer on the bar car. First thing you know, you're hooked on tranquilizers. You're not a Lush any more. You've lost Identity, become a Cipher.

The principal trouble with tranquilizers (and why W.L. shuns them) is that they are taken alone, with a lousy glass of water. There are no deferential bartenders, no gleaming glassware, no women to contemplate, no baseball talk, no interesting fights.

As to subsidiary medicines, these few words. Always cram your body with thiamine (for your nervous system), food (for your liver), and raw carrots (for your night vision). Aspirin, too, can prove a helpful agent, for it will cure almost anything and, taken in sufficient quantity, will cure Everything.

Every Man His Own Westmore

Cosmetics are an important, though furtive, part of the hungover man's successful morning. Murine works, should be used at all times. (*Murine* is a family word, so the bottle can safely be left in the desk.) The astringent for the cheek is permitted every one, but must be left at home in the bathroom cabinet. "Erace," "Covermark," and similar devices for camouflage of bumps, booze blossoms, and bruises present no problems of concealment. Select *your* shade and buy the most outrageously feminine tube in the store. Tie a ribbon around it and it becomes a gift. You can leave it right in the top drawer of your desk.

If you manage to catch an early train, a good facial before venturing to the office creates the psychic momentum to carry you through the morning. If the facial is topped by a prolonged stay under the sunlamp, you can explain away bleary eyes and a rotten flush by saying, "Got too damn much sun at the barbershop this morning." *Sun* and *barbershop* are okay words and should be used as frequently as possible, anyway.

I Hear You Calling Me

As the career lush will realize at once, this brief section deals not with answering when people call, but with *not* answering when people *don't* call.

The hungover man is desperately subject to the biddings of his unconscious, and frequently suffers minor hallucinations therefrom. On one particularly bad morning, W.L. bought a pair of sunglasses and wore them on his way to the office. In his brief ten-block purposeful canter, he distinctly heard a familiar voice call out, "Hey, W.L., whatya got the shades on for?" And later, "W.L., you been on a bat?" Did Our Hero stop, turn, and peer around for his tormentor? Certainly not. He strode on, ever onward, to his office. In the course of his journey, however, he realized the wisdom inherent in this aural hallucination and discarded the shades in a litterbasket. Later, he wondered at ever having bought them. For he knew that sunglasses, like shoes without laces, are for men who have time for vanity, and not for the Working Lush.

Visual hallucinations are another matter entirely. We speak here not of floorsful of bats, frogs, spiders, snakes, and similar unfriendly visitors whose appearance signals that it is time to Dry Out. We are discussing the small, everyday hallucinations such as Spots.

Realism dictates that the Lush will see spots before his eyes at least one morning a week. Our advice is this: *Don't swing at them!* Nobody else sees them. They may see spots of their own, but they are not where your spots are. Your hand pawing around in space is a fearful giveaway. Don't even watch your spots, for they tend to move up and away, and in the middle of a meeting you will be discovered goggling stupidly at a corner of the ceiling.

A secondary visual difficulty resulting directly from The Art is double vision. Years ago, executives had to know how to read. In those days it was (and probably still is, who knows?) impossible to read a page when one had double vision, without shutting one eye. This accounted for the great popularity of the eye-patch and the monocle in pre-organization-man business. Happily, modern business is so arranged that nobody nowadays really needs to know how to read.

In cases of emergency, however, W.L. (whose vision still might test out at 20-20 if he dared try it) employs a useful prop. Years ago, he acquired a pair of plain lenses. Confronted by an importunate secretary with a document he is expected to read, W.L. removes the spectacle case from an inside pocket, dons the glasses, takes them off again, holds them up to the light, polishes them with much fanfare. Putting them on once again, he squints at the document and then gently massages one eye with his index finger. This ploy accomplishes the double objectives of creating sympathy for his apparent myopia and reducing that spot awaiting his signature from two blank lines to one.

Meeting Management

From time to time, there will be announced, at the dangerous hour of, say, 10:00, a meeting which you cannot avoid. If you are not absolutely Restored, resort to the medications listed under "CHEATING." If, however, you are in any shape at all, seize the occasion of the meeting as an exercise in deceit.

Start on top. That is, take the initiative. Open bluff, hearty, with, "Well, it looks like everybody's here. *What's on the agenda this morning?*" In the congenial murmurings that follow, maintain a benign silence. You have already indicated that Somebody Else must begin if there is to be any meeting at all.

When the occasion of the meeting is established, make some perfectly senseless comment. "That's not really insurmountable. What do *you* think, Jeb?" Now Jeb is committed to talk, making relative sense, for five minutes. If there is a Journeyman Drunk in the room who is suffering his apprenticeship, nail him. Regard him with sudden, keen interest and say, "Lloyd looks like he's just had some idea hit him. What is it, Lloyd?"

Lloyd then clears his throat and begins. "I was think-ing...." is voice congeals on the difficult "ing" sound, he raises a trembling hand to touch a soft spot on his fore-head, looks about in desperation, and coughs, softly but deeply.

W.L.:	(moving in) Correct me if I'm wrong, Lloyd, but that was a background paper, wasn't it, Old Boy, you were getting up on the Armco account?
Lloyd:	Well...the girls in the typing pool... they....
Chairman:	(remembering no such background paper, if indeed there ever was one) Uh, yes, Lloyd, didn't you field that one at our last meeting?

| W.L.: | (taking charge, for his only time at bat) As soon as you can arrange to have that circulated to the Executive Committee, Lloyd.... |

If Lloyd is less than a man, he may burst into tears at this point.

In the course of the meeting, snipe. Snipe gently so as not to be put in the position of making a harangue to defend yourself. (The harangue places strain on poise.) A quiet chuckle, a mild snort, an occasional hearty slogan—all establish that you are present and awake, yet commit you to no embarrassing contributions.

Finally, close the meeting yourself. This too, establishes your presence and requires nothing of you. "Well, I guess that does it, eh, Joel?" is effective. If, miraculously, something has Been Decided in the meeting, sigh and say, "I wish all our problems were this easy," and walk slowly out, a heavily burdened figure, evoking admiration not untinged with pity.

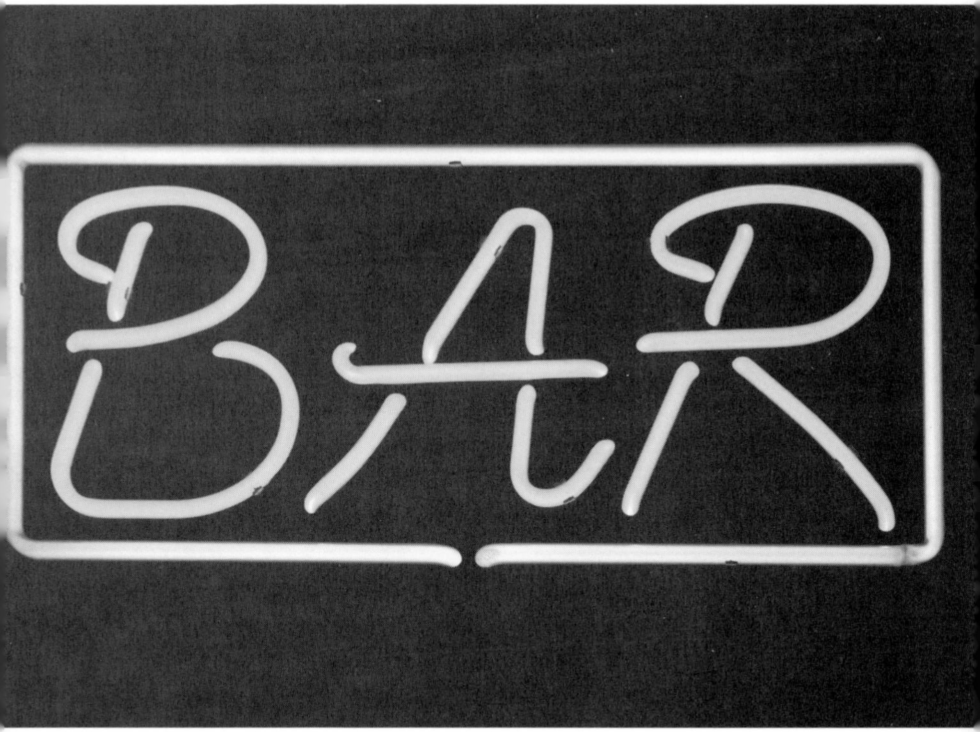
BAR

Chapter Five

ELEVEN-TWENTY

To date in this work, we have mentioned 11:20 several times, without explanation. This was done for purposes of brevity, on the assumption that every Working Lush, however naive, knows that 11:20 is the hour at which he gets his First Drink, or Fix.

A few words, then, about 11:20. First, never look forward to it or it may not come. Don't be a clock-watcher. Learn the secret thrill of discovering that it is 11:23 and that you have not tormented yourself all morning in anticipation.

It is 11:20, let us say. Time for the first belt. How is this first belt accomplished?

The Bottle in the Desk

Common sense dictates that the bottle in the desk is a Bad Thing. Others may discover it. The Working Lush has a high degree of absenteeism, however neatly he disguises its cause. In his absence, all kinds of Enemies will see fit to rummage about in his desk. Discovering a bottle, they will devise some occasion to make this fact outrageously public. Yet the bottle in the desk is clearly a logistical necessity. What to do?

In the first place, be sure that the bottle in your desk is Good Stuff. While a bottle of cheap rye can seem perfectly lovely to a man who needs a drink, it can repel (and move to vocal action) a non-lush Informer. So make this bottle a good one. Fine Scotch or bourbon, even when come upon unexpectedly and out of context, looks like *money* to the viewer. Seven or eight dollars worth of money, which speaks well for anybody. And keep the bottle half full, at least, *at all times*, for that introduces the possibility that it has been there a long time and hardly touched at all.

One solution to the Bottle-in-the-Desk problem that comes immediately to mind is the wrong one. The Aspirant thinks at once to disguise his hooch in a bottle of cough medicine. Three things are wrong here. One, some Paul Pry will open that medicine bottle during your absence and sniff it. Two, most cough-medicine bottles are small and do not hold enough booze for a Fix. Three, medicine bottles are slippery, elusive, not made to slap your hand around and drink from. Suppose some morning you fall a-trembling at 11:20 and drop the damned thing. Then your office stinks for a week, and you acquire the reputation of a Closet Drunk.

W.L. has a nice solution to the Bottle-in-the-Desk dilemma. He has a fifth of Good Stuff gift-wrapped according to season (Christmas wrappings in the spring, Easter-bunny paper in the fall, etc.). He slices the top of the gift box on three sides and secures the lid with transparent tape, lifting and reclosing the lid when he needs a Fix. On the outside of the package is a small card reading, "To W.L. From all the guys at the gym." That label says a lot about W.L. More important, the wrapping is six months out of season. That bottle has obviously been there since Easter or since Christmas, or since the most distant holiday season. That booze means so little to W.L. (the Spy is convinced) that he's never bothered to take it home.

The Bar in the Office

In time, you will achieve eminence in the corporate structure. You will be given a Corner Office with a Bar. This would seem to solve everything. Not at all. Rather, it presents new challenges. When Management installed a Bar in W.L.'s office, it did so with the tacit but inviolable admonition that he would not be anywhere near it until 5:30. By *that* time, you say, Who Needs a Drink? You are right.

However, eminence in the corporate structure brings with it other benefits. Among these is the motion-picture projector. When things are bad, W.L. orders the projector for 11:20 and has the mailboy set it up on the Bar. Thence, from his vantage point at the bar, W.L. gets quietly drunk in the dark, watching a soothing Company Film.

Clients offer another answer to the Bar-in-the-Office problem. W.L. schedules his appointments so that he finds himself at 11:20 with a customer who needs a Fix as badly as he does but is foolish enough to Let It Show. A sample conversation between W.L. and his Drinking Client goes something like this:

W.L.: (airily, waving at the Bar with its rows of gleaming bottles) Help yourself, Leigh, if you want anything.

Leigh: (willing, unsure) Is it that time already?

W.L.: (coldly indifferent) It's 11:20.

Leigh: You going to have a little something?

W.L.: You go help yourself. I might have a glass of whisky* later on, to keep you company.

Thus, W.L. shifts the burden of guilt to his client. If he is taken very drunk later in the day, he blames the client for the shape he's in, saying, "I spent the day holding Leigh's hand, so I'm cutting out early." (Be assured that Leigh is back at *his* shop explaining to everybody who really

* Nomenclature on "a glass of whisky" is discussed under "Thesaurus" in this Guide.

matters that the agency fellows went out of their way to get him tight, and he's cutting out early.)

Nipping Out to a Saloon

Properly managed, Nipping Out is by far the best 11:20 procedure. (If you are on Outside Business, or otherwise have reason to Roam the Streets, the process is known as Nipping In.) The rules below apply in all cases.

For the man who Nips Out, the same, reason for leaving the office must obtain every day. Establish a reputation as a health nut. Talk about Gyms, and about food supplements. Then your daily 11:20 exodus is a constitutional, a brisk Harry-Truman-Hike to clear the head and lungs. If you attempt a new reason every day, nobody will be misled. One day you will, altogether at a loss, say something like; "My trousers are on fire and I'm going around the corner to the firehouse." Everybody will Laugh and there you are, job-hunting again.

In the title of this section, we have used the term "Saloon." It was used only to indicate a general source of booze. *Never* go to an ordinary Saloon or Bar & Grille for your 11:20 Fix. There is a hotel near your office. With any luck, you are surrounded by hotels, each of which has at least one bar. The bar has a street entrance, as well as a lobby entrance. Never Use the Street Entrance. Enter the hotel through its front door; enter the bar from the lobby.

Once inside the bar, adopt an attitude of icy calm. Help is at hand. This attitude need be sustained only for a matter of minutes, yet it is of incalculable worth. It creates a barrier of useful enmity between you and the barman. He will serve you your something-on-the-rocks (never a Bloody

Mary or Whisky Sour, for to hoist either is to advertise your condition) and go back to wiping the mirrors. Thus he will not learn your name—to bandy about later. He will not, further, essay any sickening intimacies about his own condition as compared with yours. He will not stand goggle-eyed witnessing your tremor.

At 11:20, you have no friends. If a co-worker is already in the saloon you have chosen to enter, *do not flee*. Walk to the bar and ask for change for cigarettes. Then start a conversation with your colleague. Make an elaborate show of not looking at his drink; forget to buy the cigarettes because you are so upset at seeing him in this condition; and go on to the next hotel for your Fix.

Suppose you are standing at the bar with a drink in your hand and one of your fellows walks in. This is a tough situation. No dogma will suffice. But certainly your behavior must be flexible, dictated by the status of the Intruder. Some examples:

Mailboy:	Stare coldly. If he feels compelled to speak or smile, nod forbiddingly to him.
Equal:	(Who is a Citizen) "Come on over and say hello, John. I've been doing a little firsthand research on this whisky business. Now this store...."
Equal:	(Who is a Lush) "What happened, Emerson, you running out of hotels?"
Board Chairman:	(Successful Working Lush) "Sherlock Holmes said there was no cure

for enteric but whisky and I'll try anything. You having something for your malaria?"

Board Chairman: (Citizen) "Here for an early lunch, C.B.? Mind if I join you? I must say I find it more efficient to beat the crowd in these places."

After you have had a Fix, your breath will smell of alcohol. Take something for it. Sen-sen is out now, and always has been. It smells louder than gin. Chlorophyll products turn your tongue green, a symptom easily detected at forty paces. Ordinary peppermint candies are excellent. Best of all, include in your office collection of plants a small mint bush. Then you can sit at your desk and nibble its lovely leaves.

A word of caution: After the 11:20 Fix, go directly back to the office. Resist the temptation to loiter and really get Straightened Out. Remember, lunch is not far away. The rest of the drinking day is downhill.

Chapter Six

LUNCHEON MANAGEMENT-I

"LAUGH AND THE WORLD LAUGHS WITH YOU," the saying goes, "eat and you blow your Fix." Inherent in that pithy slogan is the one critical message we have concerning lunch. To wit: EAT. Always eat as much as you think will stay down. There are several reasons for this, two of them vital.

The first is Liver Damage, a long-range consideration which the practicing lush at every level of achievement keeps in an unsleeping corner of his mind. It is malnutrition, not booze, that rots the liver right out of you. Keep it fed.

The second is The Long Haul. When will your next meal be ingested? Who knows? There may be a full moon at 7:02. You will fluff the train and make a Night of It. If you have had no lunch, you'll find yourself running out of steam at 9:30. You'll be yawning over black coffee, napping in taxis. What kind of a Night of It is *that*?

All further considerations of Luncheon Management are secondary to the first commandment (Eat!), but let's inspect a few of them, anyway.

Choice of Saloon

The selection of a luncheon saloon relates intimately to the level of business achievement. For the Aspirant, of paramount import is the question, Do they extend credit? Next, Will they cash checks and hold on to the paper until it is good? If these matters are in order, you have Found A Home.

For the Working Lush high on the corporate ladder, related but different considerations obtain. Does the saloon honor credit cards? Are the monthly bills aggregated, arriving free of disastrous entries marked "Bar" or "Bev."? If so, the place may be adopted as the Home Saloon.

If you are any kind of a lush at all, you have been lunching at the same saloon for years. One gets fond of the Staff, in its saintly perseverance, and of the Management, in its role of Banker. Change Home Saloons only as promotions come your way and there are fewer people checking your expense account.

W.L. has been lunching at the same saloon *and at the same table* since he made vice-president seven years years ago. He has an arrangement with a kindly old Syrian waiter named Carl wherein he overtips (*i.e.*, bribes) Carl, and Carl responds to W.L.'s every preposterous order by bringing a martini.

When is Lunch?

You have already had a Fix at 11:20, thus there is no urgency about getting to a saloon for lunch. Wait until everybody else has left the office (making sure they see that you are still working, while *they* have time for lunch), then leave a message with the switchboard girl that you're "…grabbing a sandwich at the corner, then running over to Union Carbide."

Apart from its many obvious advantages, this tactic insures that you will miss the frantic First Sitting at your saloon and can drink and dine in the leisurely Second Sitting.

Luncheon Companions

The ideal luncheon companion is a fellow Working Lush (1) Who can write you off on his expense account;

or, (2) Whom you can write off on your expense account. With luck, you know one man in each category. If the gods have truly smiled, you know several men in the first category, which means you are a Journalist.

Lunch with a fellow lush requires no generalship. You both know what you're doing. You can relax and Talk Shop: Who's at Baldpate or Dropkick's or the Hartford Retreat; who's broken Rule Two and is going around telling anybody who'll listen that he's an alcoholic; who's dead. If only every afternoon could be passed thus! But it can't. There are the Others who must be taken to lunch.

For reasons which will become apparent, the Social Drinker makes the worst possible luncheon companion. This is the type who cannot bring himself to say, "I am a lush." (He generally ends up at AA meetings relating sordid stories from a largely mythical past). The Social Drinker requires more generalship than a Christmas-party tenor. After a few drinks, he grows voluble, erotic, and occasionally and unfortunately, aggressive.

He *can* be controlled. Let your mind slide back to the days when you, too, thought of yourself as an S. D. Then when he announces that he is going to the checkroom for cigarettes, pick up the full pack before him on the table and stuff it in his pocket. Point out that he is quite drunk and a little randy; that the checkroom girl is a grandmother (possibly his own); and that in any case she will be not at all interested in how he'd love to spend a rainy afternoon. Be firm. At this point he needs and wants Leadership.

Later, of course, he will turn on you. Since the Staff is on your pay roll, there is nothing at all to worry about. But rather than make a Scene, idly knock his drink into his lap and apologize at once. The shock will make him forget what it was he was quarreling about; the chill will cool the fires of his alcoholic passion; and the waste of booze will dissolve his anger in tears.

One sort of chap who makes a good luncheon companion is the Crowd Pleaser, or Holiday Drunk. Unbelievable as it may seem, this man loses his taste for booze between Occasions. He is, nonetheless, a pretty good hang-in-there drinker when the Thirst is upon him. He will get thirsty on St. Patrick's Day, on any day between December 15 and January 5, and on a Feast Day of your device entitled "Our Annual Drunk."

The Crowd Pleaser can be a lot of fun for lunch. He knows a host of stories not current in saloons. And he always means it when he reaches for the check. That's the kind of man he is. Damn shame there aren't more of them.

Women Drunks

If anything in the world is worse than Social Drinkers as luncheon companions, it is Women Drunks. They cannot talk baseball or saloons. You must not talk Sex with them or they may Take You Up On It. However, if there are no other suitable drinking companions around for lunch—or you simply find yourself trapped with a Woman Drunk—apply these rules:

1. Do not mention your wife, or she will tell you all about her bum of a husband.

2. If she has no children, tell her all about yours. That will shut her up.

3. Do not mention the name of any writer. Be particularly careful not to mention the name of a writer whose work you admire. She will have a long and distressingly detailed story to tell you about that writer's Sex Life.

4. *Do* tell long, dull stories about yourself in some utterly masculine environment (the Army, prep school, the sea). She cannot counter with stories about women because she doesn't know any women.

Martinis

The martini is a very gauche drink. W.L.'s secretary, when she and the girls have a shower-lunch, orders a martini, great with olive.

But gauche or not, the martini in quantity is the drinker's drink, and it is to martinis that W.L. turns before lunch. To order several at a sitting, however, is to brand oneself publicly as a lush. There are certain devices to circumvent this. The idea, in each case, is to get that mart *without ordering it aloud*.

1. Bribery, or Fraud: In your Home Saloon, that waiter is on your pay roll. Don't forget it and don't let him forget

it—which is to say, Keep Those Tips Coming! Arrange that when you order some drink with a perfectly silly name, a White Baby or a Maiden's Prayer, he serves a tall, frosted glass, filled with ice cubes, a small portion of dry vermouth, and a half-pint of gin. All this is garnished with lemon peel and a bloody *bush* of parsley. Be sure that with a Nancy drink like that in your fist, you will never be spotted for a lush.

2. Indirection: Make a lunch date with a noted martini lush. When asked if you'd like a drink, point to his glass and say, "That looks pretty good. What is it?"

"A martini."

"What does it taste like?"

"A martini." (shrugging)

"I'll try one of those. How are potato futures?"

Indirection can also be used at cocktail parties. Go right up and introduce yourself to the first martini lush you can find. When your host appears and asks you what you'd like, point at the mart lush's drink and say, "Anything at all. One of those would be fine."

There are circumstances and conditions in which the martini is taboo:

—When you are thirsty, for the martini will quench your thirst and everything else with it.

—When they are free, because successful martini drinking requires an Arcaro-like sense of pace. The availability of martinis, free and in quantity, unhinges this sense of pace. You won't make it to the quarter pole.

—When you are in a moving vehicle (bar car, champagne flight, or driving to New Haven for the Game). You will arrive at your destination Smashed, although the reasons for this are not known. If you are in motion, and you want to arrive with a little Edge (for the Game, perhaps, in order not to be too shy to cheer), drink Mothersill's and tonic, twist of lime.

—Through a straw. Don't ask questions! Just don't drink gin through a straw. For that matter, and in the same vein, don't fall from high places; don't fraternize with tarantulas; don't drink the house dry on Saturday night.

—When you are in the dark. Never, never, never, drink martinis in the dark. They are all the trouble you need in broad daylight.

Chapter Seven

LUNCHEON MANAGEMENT-II

WE HAVE, THUS FAR, presented lunch as a fairly simple maneuver. Fortified by his 11:20 blast, W.L. stays in the office until after 1:00, has four martinis at his luncheon saloon between 1:30 and 2:15, and eats a leisurely lunch. Actually, nothing comes that easy to the Working Lush (or he wouldn't be a lush).

To start with, the 11:20's have taken the edge off his hangover. As a result, he often approaches the restaurant at 1:30 with reluctance close to loathing. In truth, he would like nothing better than a glass of milk and a nap. The thought of laying gin into the roiling pit of his stomach fairly sickens him. Yet he does not falter.

He strides to his table, ordering in his most resolute voice: "A Shirley Temple, Carl." When his martini is served, he takes it almost at a gulp. His stomach quails, essays a rebellious regurge, then quiets, subdued, surrendering.

Where does this fortitude come from? Whence this infinite capacity for self-punishment? W.L. remembers Rule Two: *Drink one day at a time, one drink at a time.* Don't look ahead! he tells himself. Get this one down and the rest will be automatic. Man, don't you *want* to be a lush? Do you want to Lose Your Identity?

The first drink re-establishes the alcoholic process; the second confirms it; the third is nourishment for the wit; the fourth a modest aperitif while lunch is being prepared and served. By the time the fourth is downed, W.L. is back on the hook and is himself again.

The 300-Minute Hour

The phrase "lunch hour" is a distressingly cute archaism. The successful Working Lush uses it liberally, as, "I'm going shopping at Korvette's (or Macy's basement, or the

Five & Ten) on my lunch hour." Actually, nobody who is anybody has an hour-or-less for lunch. But just how long have we? How much of the company's time can decently be taken from the middle of the workday and put into a saloon?

The answer is that with proper planning you can spend as much time on any given day in a saloon as you care to. Notice we say "any given day," and not "every day." No matter how facile and valid-sounding your excuses may be, prolonged absences will force Management (a) to fire you outright; or, (b) in awe of your inventive facility, to name you Creative Director, which, as everybody knows, means you will be fired in a month.

Proper planning means the careful compilation of places where you might reasonably be, but cannot be reached by telephone. (See "CALLING IN.") For example: the Economics

Section of the public library, where they refuse to page; Vic Tanny's, where they have yet to page anyone successfully; Yankee Stadium, where they'll page only if you're a doctor or double-parked or both; and any university (N.Y.U., Fordham, Hunter), where you cannot possibly be reached.

In all circumstances, call your secretary at intervals, telling her where you are supposed to be, and assuring her that you'll be back around 5:00 to Sign The Mail. Under no circumstances leave the office without having created some useless mail (See "W.L. AND HIS SECRETARY," below), or she will curl your flesh with a stinging "Just what mail is *that?*" If Management should ask her in the course of the afternoon where you are and when you will be back, she has the answers at hand *without recourse to lies of her own manufacture.* Management can ask no more of the most ardent company man.

Not Going to Lunch

As often as the soul can endure, send out for a sandwich and coffee. Once a week would be great, but wholly unrealistic. Sending out for lunch is of value because it creates the useful illusion that you are busy, that you have Things To Do. (You have, of course, nothing to do but be Marked Present five hours a day. But the illusion of busy-ness is effective when promotions are in order.)

W.L. sends out for lunch one day a month. You can set your calendar by him. This is the day he sees his dentist for a cleaning, or for repairs to his fragile pivot teeth. Long ago, W.L. learned that if he has several drinks before seeing his dentist, the novocaine won't take. So he is content with his 11:20's and a sandwich at his desk.

After the dentist has had his will with him, W.L. retires

to a saloon for the remainder of the afternoon. Should he decide to return to his office, he covers the fact that he is Noticeably Unsteady by blaming it on the shock of a "little oral surgery." The incoherence of his speech he waves off as "novocaine lip."

How to Eat

If this little subhead seems didactic (or downright officious), there's a reason. By the time you have your martinis damped down, you care so little about the rudiments of eating that they surely will abandon you. The rudiments are, of course, Read the right side of the menu first; Order arrogantly; Make a scene when the food is served; and Overtip. Further advice includes:

1. Learn to pronounce exotic dishes in the language of the Saloon Areas, or Nations, from which they come. This

will establish you among the innocent as something of a gourmet, and will serve to explain why you are in restaurants (*sic*) all the time.

2. Alcohol dissipates the natural protein in the body. Order dishes teeming with protein, or some know-it-all in a white smock will be giving you six months to live. (W.L. always orders steak-and-eggs, though it is rarely found on menus nowadays. If you've been tipping at all well, you can have it included in the fare of your Home Saloon.)

3. You will inevitably blow your lunch on some occasion. (You *knew* this was going to happen when you paved the way for it the Night Before.) Make it to the men's room. Above all, *make it back!* Don't hide down there. Return to the table and send back not only your lunch (which obviously contained a bad clam), but everybody else's as well.

Be imperious. Abuse the *maitre*. Threaten suit. Not for a moment is anyone to suspect that your stomach has been drunk into rebellion.

4. As lunch progresses, so will your thirst. *Quench it with water.* Do not order wine or beer. They are not aids to drunkenness, but inducements to sleep.

Luncheon Conversation (Television)

Civilization being what it is, luncheon conversation frequently runs to last night's television programs. Deny having seen anything. Let it be known that your set broke down two years ago and you haven't bothered to have it fixed. Otherwise, memory will betray you into this situation:

Journeyman: Did you see Jack Benny last night, W.L.?

W.L.:	No, I missed him.
Journeyman:	Well, he did this skit about a cab driver who didn't want to take him to the railroad station....
W.L.:	(chuckling)....because saying goodbye made him cry.
Journeyman:	I thought you said you missed the program.
W.L.:	(memory flooding through) I...uh... had forgotten.
Journeyman:	Man, you're losing your grip. Do yourself a favor and lay back on the booze for a few days.

It is bad enough to be caught in a memory lapse by a fellow Working Lush or even by a Citizen (who would not understand), but to be lectured thus by a Journeyman is intolerable.

Say only that you have seen no television in ages. When luncheon partners describe what you probably watched the night before, the scene will unfold in your mind's eye to be enjoyed twice.

Luncheon Conversation (Literature)

All lushes read a lot because it's a great way to drink brandy. Again the problem is recall. Not that one forgets altogether what one has read, but rather that all those books get jumbled in memory. Was Lord Jim Wolf Larsen's first mate? Did Katherine Barclay (or was it Ingrid Bergman?) ever leave that bullfighter? Who said, "Frankly, my dear, I don't give a damn"? Was it Sidney Carton? Jack Johnson?

Rather than discuss literature at lunch, simply adopt a posture in keeping with what is expected of you. Assume those opinions you are supposed to hold. Be blithe and off-hand about writers and their work. Never stoop to levity, though. Culture is Serious Business. W.L. worked up a clever little verse that carries him nicely through all literary discussions:

Conrad wrote in intricate rhythm,
Hemingway worked with shrapnel in him,
Lewis was deeper than most people think.
Bennett Cerf is a Fink.

Scott Fitzgerald is overrated,
Kerouac is addlepated,
All of the Lardners were given to drink.
Bennett Cerf is a Fink.

John Galsworthy was elephantine,
F. Sagan was only sixteen,
James Jones *may* be the Missing Link.
Bennett Cerf is a Fink.

Note that this covers all of the opinions a man in his position *should* have.

Luncheon Conversation (Politics)

To discuss politics, it is not necessary to know anything. It is only necessary to have prejudices. The rule here is simply, *If you are not a right-of-center Republican*, become one. Thanks to the secret ballot, you can vote any way you want.

Brandying Off

"Mart up and brandy off!" goes the familiar cheer. Lest the exuberance generated by that friendly cry abridge judgment, bear in mind that brandy is a convivial drink, conducive to conversation and good fellowship. These are both nighttime, not lunchtime, boons.

The message on brandy, after lunch, is Cool It. If you are compelled by circumstance to taste a pony, take one and no more. After a second brandy, the office is a trap—no less dangerous for its seeming innocence to your addled sensibilities. Do not hedge on your solitary brandy by ordering a stinger. That is *two* brandies in any decent saloon.

If you must have more than one brandy, or if you open with stingers, do it on a day when you have not Called In in the morning. You will shortly be forced to Call In in the afternoon. And two Call In's in one day is Pressing Fortune and Not Done.

Chapter Eight

THE DOLDRUMS

ONCE YOU HAVE BRANDIED MODERATELY OFF, it is 3:15 and time to get back to the office. Two-and-one-half hours of arid afternoon stretch before you. How to kill that time, since you have nothing else to do?

Read the trade magazines. That's why there are so many of them. (Their number has increased in direct proportion to the incidence of Executive Drinking.) An intensive study of *Home Improvement Dealer* will kill a half-hour. (Do not read *Advertising Age*. Its editors include a lot of cheesecake, which will induce Eroticism and impede Composure.)

Apart from afternoon meetings (where you must deceive Large Numbers of people concerning your condition), the greatest challenge in the doldrums is Fooling Your Secretary.

W.L. and His Secretary

Management provides the executive with a secretary so she can keep tabs on him. She is a Spy. Recognize this fact. Do not be disarmed by irrelevancies such as Efficiency, Cheerfulness, or Beauty.

This is not to say that your Secretary has a pipeline to Management. She doesn't. But she has been trained to communicate (in a number of ingenious ways) the fact that she has had absolutely nothing to do for a week. Knowing the forms this communication takes will prepare you to frustrate it. Here they are:

She Cleans Her Desk. By this we mean a Thorough Cleaning—not just tidying up. Management *understands* that from time to time there must occur (inevitably) a lapse in your ability to "make work" for your Spy. Thus, "tidying up" is okay. But the Thorough Cleaning is a red flag. Don't give her time.

She "Pitches In." The alert office manager knows she really doesn't want to help the other girls. She is simply bored silly.

She starts Coming In On Time. With this, Management becomes truly alarmed. Do you realize (they say, nudging one another) that this girl has been so inactive for so long that she's afraid she'll get fired if she's late?

Clearly, work must be created for your Spy or her indolence will betray your sloth. "Making work" is a game that can kill lots of time in the afternoon. It will really light up those doldrums, *if* you play the game honestly. That is, never permit the work you invent to be in any way productive for The Company.

For example: Send her out to locate all the 1958 issues of *Super Market Merchandising.* Tell her to clip all references to "detergent hands" and paste them in a scrapbook. This is grand work. It is wholy unproductive, utterly futile, and that isn't all! Those magazines and clippings will *keep her desk beautifully cluttered for weeks!*

W.L.'s secretary was hired for her skill at typing, as well as for her talents at Espionage. He keeps her typing. All second-class matter is answered with long, formal negatives. (Every ten days, for example, he declines a subscription to *Time* with a thoughtful treatise on modern politics.) When the final letters are presented for his signature, W.L. corrects the smallest error with a paintbrush in red ink. This assures there will be no simple erasures.

Errands are a nice way to keep your secretary busy because it is legitimate, in terms of the game, to make them productive for *yourself* (as opposed to The Company). Send her shopping for propitiatory offerings for your wife, rewards for your children (reminders that they have a Daddy, like other kids), and anything else you don't feel like chasing after yourself. In manufacturing errands, think always of the West Side and Downtown. Those will consume her entire afternoon. (A prime advantage of the errand is that it assures your secretary will be frequently absent from her desk. She is no longer, therefore, an effective Spy, and thus of little value to Management. First thing you know, she's safe for firing. Presto! You have six months before a new Spy learns that, aside from being on the payroll, you are otherwise unemployed.)

Creative Writing

Apart from the resumes he must indite when he is forced to change jobs, W.L. is called upon to write creatively in one circumstance only: his expense account, or

Sheet. When the doldrums are upon him, he is drunk and thus at his most inventive. He uses this period to *create* a reasonable Sheet. First of all, he is voluble and explicit. He tells the *whole* story. He also remembers to tighten up that Sheet in the bitter light of morning, before submitting it to Accounting. (Once, before he had made this safeguard habitual, he sent in a Sheet listing two such profitable and hopeful items as "rental of diving bell—$900.00," and "hasheesh for bearers—$120.00.")

From time to time you will find it difficult to Think Things Up, so keep close at hand the following list of rules:

1. Include all customary categories—transportation, lunch, hotel, drinks, dinner, and Other Entertainment (call girls).

2. Go through your address book. Under each category fill in the names of people with whom it is altogether

possible you might have had lunch, or drinks, or dinner, or Other Entertainment. (Go through the address book backward. This will assure that the names are not noticeably alphabetical on your Sheet.)

3. Ask your secretary for a copy of your Itinerary (*i.e.*, cities you were supposedly visiting during recent Bats). Kill the afternoon by thinking up appropriate hotel bills, airline fares (Remember: *round* trip!), laundry and cleaning bills. It is of value, from time to time, actually to go out of town, for then you will have vouchers to produce on Accounting's demand. If you produce vouchers just once in a while, it creates the handy impression of honesty—which impression is of use when, as is usually the case, you have no vouchers and you promise to Look For Them.

4. Keep a list of obscure categories and use them with discretion. "Purchase of Books & Publications" is rarely

contested. "Police Protection" is a nice one, especially in New York and Chicago, where the police are notoriously venal. "Emergency Medical Expenses" has not yet been turned back by any accounting department. It means you were working so hard for The Company on the road that you had an attack (enteric) and had to see a doctor.

5. When your Sheet is so utterly insupportable that you don't want anyone to read it (calling you Liar and Fool), *move the decimal point.* Accounting always reads the final figure first, then checks out the categories. So: Suppose you make an altogether absurd demand on The Company, not having laid out a penny of your own. Change, for example, $130.00 to $1300.00. Shortly after you have submitted your Sheet, the Head (it will be he, none other) of Accounting will call and say, "W.L.? I've got a personal expense account from you here amounting to $1300.00."

W.L.:   Thirteen hundred dollars! Are you serious?

Head: That's what it says. I've got it here before me.

W.L.:   Oh, Christ. That stupid girl must have moved the decimal point. I only put in for $130.00.

Head: I kind of thought it was something like that, Sir. Sorry I had to bother you. I'll sign this right away and put it in the works.

Thus, the expense account is okayed without being read. W.L. has netted a hundred and thirty bucks for the few hours spent typing up his own Sheet.

Finally, W.L. never uses "Miscellaneous." Bookkeepers don't know much, but they know this: any Sheet with an item marked "Misc." is turned back at once to the department from which it came. It makes no difference how small that miscellaneous figure is, back it goes. And someone always feels compelled to go over the whole batch of lies, not understanding that the Sheet has been turned back for the old "Miscellaneous" reason. (Now and then you can use *Miscellany* and hope to blind them with your footwork, but it is chancy.)

Resumes are another matter entirely. Here it is important *not* to be voluble, *not* to tell the whole story. Understate.

W.L. has worked for many (by definition) Very Large Firms. (Only Very Large Firms can afford him and are big enough for him to hide in.) When he constructs a new resume, he lists only these firms. These corporate eminences march in brittle majesty across the page. (Remember: The resume is only there to open doors for you. If *those* names won't do it, nothing will.)

Do not list references on your resume. Say only, "References on request." If they are indeed requested, you will have time to think of something. Chances are you won't want to work for a man you can't baffle on first meeting, anyway.

The Life of the Meeting

Afternoon meetings have nothing in common with morning meetings (See "MEETING MANAGEMENT") except, perhaps, inconclusiveness. In the morning, you force yourself to speak short, occasional sentences, so as to be Marked Present without being tricked into lengthy discourse.

In the afternoon, the impulse to Take Charge of the meeting is terribly strong. Much seems clear to you that all the others are missing badly. You have an overwhelming desire to Sum Things Up and get the meeting over with. Don't. If it all seems very clear and simple, it is because you are drunk and have forgotten half the difficulties.

There is also a temptation to fill a lull in the meeting

with a couple of small stories you happened to hear at lunch. Again, don't. For you will fall incoherent, everyone will fail to get the story because you told it all curly, and you will find yourself roaring with laughter in the midst of utter silence. Everybody will look at everybody else and nod. The jig is up.

While maintaining maximum silence in afternoon meetings, you are likely to encounter a corollary problem: that of Staying Awake. Since you are forbidden to inflict pain on yourself in public meeting ("You got leprosy, W.L.? That pencil's stuck a half-inch into your calf!"), you Play Games. Spot a bleary co-worker and call on him for his opinion on everything that comes up. Keep him talking (which he will be perfectly willing to do) until it dawns on him that he is not making sense. After he subsides, clock the intervals between nods as he slides off to sleep.

Try counting the number of times the President says "We." Analyze the doodling on either side of you for Freudian symptoms. Estimate the total salary waste for The Company (per annum) in meetings such as this.

Any game will do, so long as you Stay Awake.

Eroticism

In the doldrums you are drunk and have nothing to do. Left to its own devices, the alcoholic unconscious, always close to the surface, will erupt with gaudy obscenities. Fight them back. Tend your plants, read trade publications aloud, call a crony, go down for coffee.

All this eroticism is so much stewing in your own juice. You have your vice. You are a Lush. Actually, you're better off. It is very difficult to fit a girl, however willing, into the lower right-hand drawer of your desk.

Chapter Nine

A LITTLE SOMETHING
FOR THE TRAIN

AFTER 5:00, THE COMPANY has no further claim to you. You may drop the wearisome mask of Citizenship. The knowledge that you are through *making* money for the day and can now set about *spending* it brings a dangerous exhilaration. Guard your impulses carefully; lie back. Deliverance is at hand.

In the first place, don't leave before 5:25. True, you are no busier at 5:00 than you have been all day, but sit tight. Send your secretary along with a cheery, martyred "No point both of us working late." If, at 5:20, the President finds you sitting at your desk doing nothing, assure him with a hearty laugh that you're as eager to get going as he is, but you're waiting for a call from Chicago. Add, blithely, "Nothing my gal couldn't have handled, but she had a date so I let her go early."

Around 5:30, it is time to have a Little Something for the Train. (There is a bar car on the train, or you wouldn't be taking it. On the bar car, you have a Little Something for the Scene at Home.) With frequent tired sighs, cast off your burden of work and head for one of the many, many Saloons available to you at the cocktail hour.

Any Old Saloon

The martini in quantity, it has been noted, is the lush's drink at lunch. In the evening, with a possible Long Haul ahead, prudence dictates a change. What you change to doesn't matter. It can be Scotch or imported beer or rye with a pinch of Angostura as a stomachic. The important thing is to *get off martinis*.

Now any damn fool can make a Scotch-and-water as well as the best bartender in town. It therefore makes no difference which saloon you seek out for your cocktail Fix. Here is the opportunity to scout around for new Home Saloons against the day when your bar bill at your current Home becomes outsized.

In general, start with the best. A Scotch at "21" costs no more than the same drink on Third Avenue. (Keep your wits about you, however, if you're drinking with a Woman Drunk and decide to Make a Night of It. Otherwise, you will order food and inflict permanent damage on your fiscal planning. For the price of dinner at "21" you can go on a three-day Bat in Harrisburg.)

After 5:30, your choice of saloon is considerably broadened by the fact that it is okay to be *seen*. You can go to the bar that the Boys in the Office go to every night. There is nothing to hide. Even if you are suddenly taken drunk, it doesn't matter. You've been working too hard, you explain the next day. You were tense. The first drink hit you like a ton of bricks. (No need to mention that you had the first drink six hours earlier, at 11:20.)

Having a Drink with Chuck

Of the many effective dodges W.L. uses to screen the fact that he is getting a Fix, perhaps the best is the Business Cocktail Meeting. He makes a date with a fellow lush whose relationship is that of client, or purchaser. Then, he remarks to the Executive Vice-President that he is "having a drink with Chuck," and invites him along. More often than not, he accepts. W.L. now has opportunity not only to get his Fix on The Company's money, but he will be dealing with E.V.P. out of his native medium, Commerce. (By contrast, W.L. is in *his* native medium, Saloons.)

In the Saloon, W.L. is boss, strategist, host. He pumps more drinks into E.V.P. than he can conceivably hold. In a word, he gets him drunk. Then, he starts him talking about The Company. Unspeakable plots, ambitions, conflicts, and bitternesses pour forth. (W.L. listens carefully to all of it. There may be one little nugget of knowledge that will make him forever Indispensable.) Next, he gets him into trouble and out of it, smoothing things over nicely. (In the morning, E.V.P. is desperately guilty about his drunkenness, hopelessly in his debt, and aware that W.L. has enough on him to blackmail his way to a sinecure.

W.L. and Chuck *know* that no honest business ever gets done at the Business Cocktail Meeting. So they talk Sex and How Lousy Things Are at Home. All of this is written off on the expense account.

The Sex Hoax

During the cocktail hour, Woman Drunks of every feather abound. It is the easiest thing you know to make a date with a Woman Drunk at 5:45. They are All Over Town, hanging around their telephones, waiting for somebody, anybody, to ask them for a drink.

After he has made a date with a Woman Drunk, W.L. noises it all over the Upper Echelon. Generally, he drops by the Chairman of the Board's office waiting for him to say, "How about a little something for the train, W.L.?"

W.L.: (smiling boyishly, head bowed) I'd love to, C.B., but I made this stupid date....

C.B.: (who up to now has thought of W.L. exclusively as a drunk) Oh-ho! Got a Little Something Going for You, hey?

W.L.: Girl I haven't seen in a hundred years. Used to date* her before I got married. She called this afternoon....

C.B.: (gay dog manner) I wouldn't want to cut in on that!

W.L.: (chuckling) Frankly, C.B., I'd rather go for a drink with you—although you're nowhere near as pretty. But I think I have a little obligation here.

In this way, W.L. establishes himself as a figure of some romance, rather than a Drunk. More important, he creates the useful illusion that he has a healthy interest in Sex. That

---

* "Date" as a verb is a tidy anachronism. If you have the guts, say you were "Pinned" to the girl once.

helps to explain the "Other Entertainment" expenses on his Sheet. (See "CREATIVE WRITING.")

One fascinating aspect of having cocktails with a Woman Drunk is that you can talk her favorite subject (sex) without fear of her Taking You Up On It. (You've *got* to make that 7:02.) When a Woman Drunk starts talking sex, everybody else should start taking notes. Just about everything that can be wrong with her *is* wrong with her. That's why she is a Woman Drunk. She blames everything on her several husbands. To make the blame stick, she makes her charges wonderfully detailed. It's most fun of all if you know two or three of her former husbands, because then you can Identify—and later, possibly, Blackmail.

Watch her closely, however, as she ingests her alcohol. At one point in the evening she will either turn Mean, or turn on the Waterworks. Mean you can handle simply by calling for the check and leaving her there. But Waterworks? Ah, then you're trapped! You simply cannot walk away from a crying jag that takes place in public. (Amateurs do not seem to realize that all this sobbing is simply a side effect of alcohol. They think you have done something Terrible to hurt the woman!) If you walk away you are a rotter. What to do? Be solicitous but firm. Call for the check. Escort her to a cab. Then head for the 7:02. The next morning, she'll be on your phone, all apologies. And you can handle *that*.

The Home Saloon

If you have nothing else in the world to do at 5:30, you may find yourself in your Home Saloon. This can be dangerous. The bartender has been behind that stick (with all that free Sauce) since 11:00 in the morning. Naturally, he is drunk. This may embolden him to intimate usage. He may call you by your first name. This is, of course, Very Bad. Others of importance to you might chance into the Saloon and overhear. And *understand* all.

You cannot simply say, "Do *not* call me by my first name," or, "*Mister* Lush to you, Buster." He is Your Bartender. You *need* one another. So you cut him short. He is Stiffed, as opposed to Tipped. His views on the women at the bar (never accurate, anyway) are not sought. When volunteered, they are discredited. Soon Your Bartender is back in his place. You are "Mister" again.

The only exception to the Call-Me-Mister Rule is the Saloon Owner. He is permitted intimate usage because he foolishly permits limitless credit and cashes your paper. He is your Banker. It is okay to be on first-name terms at the Bank.

Chapter Ten

A NIGHT OF IT

AT LEAST ONCE A WEEK, W.L. says to himself, "To hell with the 7:02; I shall take a later train." Even as he says it, he knows he will *not* take a Later Train. He will make a Night of It. (The knowledge that there *are* later trains assuages his guilt. All night long, as he cabs from one Saloon to another, he consults his timetable, promising himself to be on the 8:56, the 9:41, and so on until the 2:15 has been thoroughly missed and he is in town for keeps.)

The preservation of minimum domestic felicity requires one (1) phone call home. When the phone rings at or about 7:00, W.L.'s wife knows she is not going to see him for twenty-four hours. While she may affect dismay, her first feeling is one of enormous relief. She has a night off! Tradition (and her morale) require, however, that a suitable

excuse be presented. In making these excuses, there are several things to remember.

Principally, involve the wife in your excuse. "Conway's baby is dying, and I'm filling in for him," is excellent because she identifies with Mrs. Conway and feels absolutely Stricken. If it happens to be Thursday, tell her you are staying in town to do a "little shopping" for her and the kids. (Remind her that the stores are open late on Thursday.) In the morning, send your Secretary out to do the actual purchasing. "I'm having dinner with the Dean of Admissions at Yale. Old friend of mine. He says he can get our Bill in, in spite of his high school record." (This last embodies the best of all vital elements: wife, children, your shared concern for their future, and a distinguished and presumably sober dinner companion.)

Do *not* use the customary business excuses. "L.T. and I

are working late. We're going to dinner now and I'll be on a late train," is terrible. She knows L.T. is a Lush and a Lecher because he got drunk at the Hershey convention and spent all night at her side, gauging her cleavage. Besides, business excuses are futile. The wife knows you don't do anything for The Company but endorse pay checks. Asking her to believe that you're working late is an abuse of her Understanding.

Dinner?

The answer to the eternal question, Dinner? is *Yes*. In fact, it is an imperative. A Night of It can last to 4:00 A.M., when the saloons close. Or to 8:00 A.M., when the after-hours joints spill you forth into the sunlight. You need food both to forestall liver damage and to sustain you in the Long Haul ahead. (See "LUNCHEON MANAGEMENT-I.")

Unlike lunch, dinner can get out of hand. It can be

fearfully expensive. If you fall in with Bad Company (big spenders), or succumb to the pleadings of a Woman Drunk, you may find yourself studying a tedious and outrageous menu in a supper club. To avoid this, keep several cheap and off-beat places in mind. "I know where we can get a terrific bowl of chili," can lead otherwise sane businessmen into a nowhere Mexican Saloon on the West Side. "Let's have a hamburger at the bar and then go to Nino's. I can't stand music while I'm eating," will quell the most ardent Woman Drunk because it is a nut comment and therefore unarguable.

If you're feeling genuinely frugal (or Tapped Out), attend a Saloon serving heavy *hors d'oeuvres*. Take in enough nourishment to sustain the Long Haul. Take with it the exhilarating knowledge that you are costing the Saloon money. Man bites dog!

The Evening: Handle, Shaft, and Shank

Once you have tamped down dinner with a few Scotches, you feel impossibly fit—better than you've felt all day—and the evening stretches pleasantly before you. During the evening, you will encounter many of the same people you dealt with at lunch: the Fellow Lush, the Journeyman, the Crowd Pleaser, the Woman Drunk. These you know how to handle. You will also encounter three new breeds. They are: (1) the Woman who is not a Drunk; (2) the Business Type related to, but different from, the Crowd Pleaser; and (3) Night People. Where you go and what you do during the evening is determined in large measure by the nature of your company.

Women who are not Drunks are the finest company of all. They like to be taken places where there is music—or perhaps some comedy—which for you is a refreshing change of Saloon. They become damply fond after drinking hardly anything at all. They never bore you about their Bum of a Husband, because the chances are if they had (or have) a husband, they think he's a pretty nice guy.

There is this danger in the appeal of Women who are not Drunks: they can make you nostalgic for the days before you consecrated yourself to the bottle. If you're not careful, you'll find yourself making solemn vows about your Future Behavior—vows you know you will forget or ignore in the morning. This can be depressing.

The Business Type who is on the town is absolutely *the* outstanding bore. Even before you have finished your first 5:30 drink, he is asking where all the girls are. He does not intimate that you are responsible for finding him some girls. He assumes it. Where this assumption comes from

(Logic? Tradition? Scripture?) is utterly unknown. But there it is. The Business Type accepts it as an article of faith.

At first, you say, "How in hell do I know where all the girls are? I'm an account executive, not a pimp." The businessman brushes this aside, saying that in another time ("When I was your age…") or another place ("If you ever get to Chicago…") he could produce lascivious beauties beyond counting.

Now and then, at the Business Type's unabating urging, you call a couple of girls and ask them to meet you. Herein you make the biggest mistake possible. For B.T. will (a) get drunk, and slap a half nelson on the prettier girl; (b) get drunk, talking nonstop for four hours about his family-and-business back in God's Country; (c) get drunk, and pick a fight with somebody for "staring at his girl."

Remember this, too. No matter how attractive or willing the girls may be, sometime during the evening the Business

Type will decide they are both Dogs, and propose "...why don't we beat it while they're still in the can?"

Night People are a breed apart. Only one generalization will serve: to a man, they are unbalanced. Beyond that, they are as varied as Day People. Some of them drink all the time; others drink scarcely at all. Some work; others do not. Some are rich, some poor; some lead, some follow. What they all have in common is the ability to *sleep days* and the compulsion to venture out only in darkness.

The Night People Lushes have nowhere near as much fun as the Day People of the same calling. The diminution of social pressure assures this. They don't have to sneak out to a Hotel Bar at 11:20. When they have been up, say, three-and-one-half hours, it is 7:30. Saloons are are booming. They get their Fix right out there in the open. When they have been up ten hours (6:00 P.M., your time), it is 2:00 in the morning.

Everybody in sight is drunk, too. There is nothing to hide. If the Daytime Lush seems, at times, to talk down to the Nighttime Lush, it is not surprising. Where are the challenges at night? Who is there to hide from? The game is gone.

Late Saloons

Occasionally with Women who are not Drunks; often with Business Types; and always with Night People, you will find yourself in the Late Saloon. A Late Saloon is a bar that a lot of people go to late at night for no discernible reason. There is no music, no entertainment; more often than not, the glassware is dingy, the drinks are ungenerous and expensive. Frequently, bartenders and waiters are too drunk to respond to your simplest order with anything but throaty laughter. (If they are not drunk, they spend their time stealing either the customers' girls or their change.)

There is no earthly reason for this Saloon to survive. No good can come of a visit there. Yet, it is full every night and will be full for many years to come. For that is how it is with Late Saloons.

Two maxims concerning Late Saloon Behavior: *Maintain Total Peace*; and *Overtip*. Night People do not have anywhere to go in the morning. Thus, temporary disfigurement causes them no embarrassment. But the Working Lush must shun any hostility that might result in, say, a discolored eye. Be sure to Overtip, because all explosive breaches of the peace are entered into with robust gaiety by the Staff. (In this way, it is established there is a Winner and a Loser, and the fight is over.) As long as you Overtip wildly, the Staff will Make A Loser out of your adversary. Isn't that worth a few dollars across the bar?

Accommodations

At 4:30 A.M., W.L. is led (or pushed) to the street. His first thought is to join the bartenders at an after-hours joint. But he has to Get Up In The Morning. An intelligent appraisal of his condition indicates he needs sleep. (Also, after-hours joints, like everything else, are not what they used to be. They are not Gay any more. Not even interesting. And they must pay immense sums to the police in order to stay open. This expense is passed directly on to the patron.)

W.L.'s second thought, therefore, is of sleeping accommodations for the few hours he has remaining before he must return to the office. If he is in the company of a sensible career lush, he can go to his (or her) place and pass out on the couch or floor. Wisely, nothing more is asked of him, for he has nothing more to give.

Alternative Accommodations

W.L. never calls a friend at 4:30, asking to be put up. He knows that in gaining a night's shelter he will lose a friend.

Rather, W.L. uses the waiting room at Grand Central. Uniformed types throw homeless men out of that room when it is cold enough to make the throwing-out worth while. Not so with W.L. The guards disturb him only to wake him at an hour he specifies. W.L. purchases a Pullman ticket to some-where (Albany, say) and asks to be awakened in time for the 9:20 train. Awed by the utter respectability of his destination and the show of affluence his ticket represents, the guards even shush passers-by so that he can sleep. Upon awakening, W.L. nips into the splendid Grand Central Men's Room for a shower, shave, shine, and a quick press for his suit. All of which he pays for by cashing in the ticket to Albany.

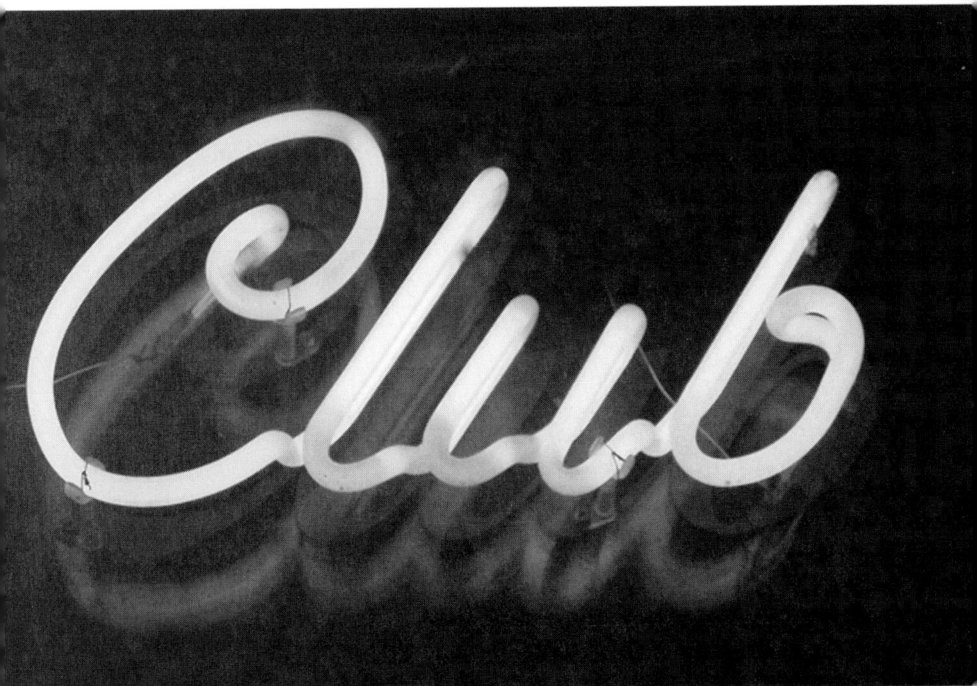
Club

Chapter Eleven

CONJUGAL LOVE

MORE OFTEN THAN NOT, you will cut short the cocktail hour and hurry like hell to catch the 7:02. This is not the hardship it might seem, for there is a bar car on the 7:02. It is the last train with a bar car. Hence the hurry.

Once in the bar car, have a Little Something for The Scene at Home. Pace yourself. Sip. Distract yourself by cheating furiously at dollar poker. (Remember: you are on a moving vehicle. Lushing while in motion is treacherous.)

Driving

Waiting for you at the station is another kind of vehicle— *automotive*. It may be a jeep you parked there in the morning; or it can be a more respectable conveyance, with your wife sitting in the right front seat. In either case, you are

called upon to Drive. That is, to summon up such near-atrophied faculties as eye-hand co-ordination, judgment, and prudence. (We distinguish between "judgment" and "prudence," because judgment frequently dictates that you drive far faster than is *prudent*. Otherwise, you will hug the curb at eight miles per hour and a Cop will spot you for a Lush.)

Give yourself a little edge on the car. Visualize the dashboard, pedals, and gear-shift before you open the door. Otherwise, you will sit stunned and groping behind the wheel. The car—sensing this lack of confidence—will refuse to start.

If you are going to be driving alone, visualize the first two or three turns you must take to get home, *before you get off the train.* This assures that when you Get Lost, you will be within hailing distance of home. They will hear you crying and come get you. If you cannot visualize the first few turns, spot a Sobersides who looks vaguely familiar and follow his car. Chances are he lives next-door to you (and is godfather to your oldest boy).

In general, the Working Lush is a safe driver. That is because he is a little bit afraid of automobiles and traffic, as he is a little bit afraid of everything else. He is dangerous only before he has had his Fix, when his nerves are no good at all. When he is involved in an accident, the case history commonly reads, "In endeavoring to avoid a leaf that fell on his windshield, deponent left road and collided with tree."

Such accidents are to be avoided. They are bad for morale. Generally, the report of the accident makes you look like a Fool. And you can't proclaim in court, "I am a Drunkard, not a Fool!" They don't seem to see the difference.

Song, Oratory, and The Dance

The Working Lush is cunning, elusive as a wounded animal. Yet more often than one would think possible he is trapped at his own front door by a strange vamp (his wife) who greets him with the news that they are to have dinner at the home of somebody duller or richer than they. With any warning at all, he would not have come home, would have stayed in town and Made a Night of It. Wife protests that she told him about the date three or four times. (In truth, she never mentioned it. After twenty years of marriage to a Working Lush, a little cunning has rubbed off.) And now will he please go up and shower and change?

He showers. He changes. He shapes up. He may feel resentment: he has been outfoxed, conned into a stagnant evening of staying on his feet, making sense, keeping awake. But he Plays it Cool. Resentment, he knows, is the mark of the Journeyman Lush. And the Journeyman's resentment flares forth in the ludicrous forms of Song, Oratory, and The Dance. W.L. has been to these Amateur Nights; he knows.

Unlike The Dance (which develops out of them), Song and Oratory start simply enough. A gay group of young marrieds gathered about a piano can launch him into Song. A chance allusion to a romantic poet will move the Journeyman to peaks of Oratory.

At the end of his opening solo, there is mild applause and milder confusion. At encore's end, there is no applause and the confusion is no longer mild. The Wife gives him the old Osprey Eye; the host presses drinks on him; the audience wanders vaguely away in silence. Rather than taming him, these evidences of disapproval cascade the Journeyman into an orgy of retaliatory exhibitionism. Song and recitation become louder, or obscene, or both. When still he is ignored, he hurls himself into The Dance. (This exertion, which will one day kill him, is composed in equal parts of the flamenco and the field goal try.)

Journeyman is in real trouble and he knows it. He is Making a Fool of Himself. He knows that, too. But he cannot stop.

At noon the next day, when Memory returns, he will burn for a time with shame. He will then console himself, remembering that James Joyce, a peerless lush, was also a devotee of The Dance when in his cups. He is further consoled in the knowledge that he did not have to beg for solo honors. With another lush about, he would have been dancing *a deux*.

The Quiet Evening At Home

W.L. and his wife rarely go out, preferring to spend their evenings quietly at home. He has long since established with her both his antisocialism and his pressing physical need for rest. "If there's one thing you can't take with enteric, it's a lot of helling around nights." (Remembering previous public occasions, she accepts the fictional limitations of his fictional ailment.) On arriving home, W.L. throws open the front door and yells, "What's for dessert?" Connoted therein is a hoard of suburban ambiance. His wife greets this witticism of long standing with a small smile, offering him a drink.

Drink in hand, W.L. turns his attention to the children. Since he need abide them only a short time (those too old to go to bed at 8:30 are Away At School), he showers them lavishly with affection, small jokes, and patience.

After the children have been tucked in, W.L. and his wife sit down for a quiet drink together. A master at spinning domestic conversation ("Time to cross-polinate the ageratum?" "What do you hear from your mother?" "Have they fixed the leak in the eaves?"), W.L. manages to keep his wife holding forth through four or five drinks. Then, while she's putting the finishing touches to dinner, he expands his topics ("Gruenther was no man for that assignment!") through a couple of extra belts.

At table, W.L. eats selectively. His liver firmly in mind, he manages to opt for whatever high protein is available. Fats, carbohydrates, and sugars are abjured. A neat black coffee closes his repast.

Later, a book firmly grasped in his left hand, W.L. rounds off the day with an ever-normal snifter of brandy at his right, and a few quiet chuckles.

Chapter Twelve

THE ENTERTAINER

RIGHT OR WRONG, Americans are gregarious, in business and out. Parties, socials, and get-togethers are the lot of nearly everybody. While some may deplore these holdovers from a frontier culture, and some even enjoy them, there is no question that to the successful Working Lush they present a real Threat.

Given a bunch of essentially awkward people, with no very clear idea of why they've been assembled, you'll find an amazing consumption of booze. It's just there that the successful lush must be on his guard. Undisciplined imbibing makes him nervous. It should. But what is he to do? On these occasions, *the Amateur Lush is in the saddle.* How to unseat him?

The Business Bust

Call it what you will (the annual meeting, the sales con-
ference, the new-product party, the convention, the regional
meeting), the Business Bust has become an institution.
Predicated on one or another phony premise, the business
gettogether is now as omnipresent as the TV Western and
the plastic bag. Ostensibly occasions for exchanging information, whipping up the sales force, or explaining away
low earnings, such functions have come to serve a single
purpose; *i.e.*, they provide an airtight excuse for millions
of people to Get Away from Home so that they can Get
Drunk. (For reasons of propriety, side action involving
Sex and Celebrations Sensual will not be discussed here.)
What, then, is our lush to do in the face of such multiplied
rank amateurism?

W.L. learned long ago that to dodge the issue was to err. Early on in his career, he volunteered to Management that he be placed in charge of the yearly sales meeting. (This event, held either in St. Petersburg or Atlantic City, depending on the most favorable off-season rates, is a Bust of no small proportion. For one thing, it gives the President his annual opportunity to engage in Oratory before a captive audience. For the Executive Vice-President, it is a once-a-year opportunity to Make It with the booze and the broads. He does.)

As Master of the Revels, W.L. has as his concern a number of matters. He handles them all well. At the Company Cocktail Party, for example, he comports himself thus:

Pres.:   (who is still on his first drink) What did you think of my little talk, W.L.?

W.L.: Just great, Chief. I kept wondering, though, if it wasn't just a mite over their heads.

Pres.: Nonsense. The PR agency that wrote it...uh, that is...I'm sure it was right on the nail.

W.L.: Right! Say, E.V.P. is enjoying himself, isn't he?

Pres.: Hadn't noticed. This meeting isn't a vacation, you know. Plenty to do here.

W.L.: It's a working meeting, if I ever saw one. Maybe we ought to close the bar. Some of the younger men....

Pres.: You're in charge, W.L. Glad to see you're on your toes.

Having shut down the Company Cocktail Party, W.L. is off to a local bar remote enough from the meeting site to insure that he won't be disturbed. Happy in the thought that he will be expense-accounting his evening's drunk, he leans into a series of Scotches, musing on the uninformed ways of the Amateur Lush.

Company for Lunch

On occasion, you will find yourself summoned to a Company Lunch. Do not despair. It means that you have been Marked for Success. Or at least that someone has made a point of knowing how to spell your name. In either case, you're on your way Up.

Most Company Lunches are held in the Executive Dining Room. This makes it a cinch. Either there is no bar (and thus no Amateur Drunks) or a white-coated waiter serves up (at the most) two warm-and-watery martinis, poured from a ready-mix bottle in the pantry. Alcohol, in short, is absent. Since you have had plenty of advance notice, you have already taken care of the problem with an exceedingly generous 11:20 Fix. Smilingly patient, you request a "ginger ale, or something like that," and make a business of complimenting the Company food. Once lunch is at an end, you are free to spend the rest of the afternoon in a saloon of your choice. Big Occasions like this send Management for a spill. No one will be around the rest of the day.

At Home With the Boss

On rare occasions, you and your wife will be invited to the President's home for a "little evening." One of the problems seen immediately here is that the evening will not be *little*. At least forty people people will be on hand. No matter. Here's your chance.

First of all, accept the fact: the rich Live Well. This means there will be a liquor supply that will both arouse your envy and shake your faith in the purchasing power of the salaried. The temptations are multitude: all that hooch; all that service; all that euphoria! Ignore them. Remember that you are as powerful as the boss, where it counts. (His Sheet cannot be half so creatively written, nor one-tenth so rewarding.) Let the Journeymen, the Amateurs exceed themselves. As for you, surprise your wife and pull all evening on a tall, wet highball that you wouldn't be caught dead with on another occasion.

Your reward for this exemplary conduct may very well be a tidy raise.

The Intruders

Besides the press of Business Social Life (which is in itself wearing enough), most of us face the prospect of Entertaining At Home. Fortunately, this kind of thing can be held to a minimum. (W.L. permits his wife an annual "Strawberry Festival," to which are invited all those petitioners who would otherwise clutter up the house with inane cocktail brawls and other loosely conceived drinking occasions.) As with other social demands, these duties cannot be shirked. To be thought an Antisocial Nut is almost as inconvenient as to be thought a Drunk.

The answer, then, is to Entertain. The device is the Cook-out.

Apart from the indignities of wearing funny hats and aprons bearing unintelligible mottoes, the cook-out has a distinct advantage: it keeps them Out! And "out" is where guests should be. Gaggling around the house, they may discover The Kitchen. The Kitchen is where you are.

Instantly the first guests arrive, shoulder them into the back yard (or patio, or terrace, or garden, or whatever in hell you call yours). Allow for no side trips or diversions along the way. Get them chairs, get them drinks, and get them talking. Keep them that way. Establish that the party is Here. (You will be grateful for this, later in the evening.)

Alongside the cooking paraphernalia (see "THE UNPRE-PARED CHEF," below) you have set up a Dummy Bar. This is simply a table, disguised under one of your wife's most outlandish "luncheon cloths," upon which you have placed an unbelievable collection of strainers, stirrers, shakers, squeezers, openers, tongs, corkscrews, picks, and other assorted "home bar" hardware. Pitchers, glasses (all sizes and shapes), napkins, and swizzle sticks abound. Mounds of lemon peel, orange slices, cocktail onions, maraschino cherries, olives, and pistachio nuts beckon invitingly. A brimful ice bucket crowns your achievement.

Somewhere in all this may be found a few bottles of inferior booze. (Here's the place for those "gift bottles" of bad Scotch and phony rye you've been handed over the year.) Beaming the role of the Hearty Host, you mix and serve these intruders a measured sequence of absolutely rotten drinks. This assures that very little drinking will be done. Certainly there will be no drunkenness, if your guests have the brains they were born with.

And that's how you want it. Drunks around the house are a problem. They Make Scenes. They may even Spy. Worst of all, *they will show up in The Kitchen.*

The Unprepared Chef

One of the truly absurd myths of our time is that food cooked out-of-doors is fit to eat. It is, as anyone who has ever experienced it knows, not *fit* for anything. A companion myth has it that the American male can cook. This is too absurd even to discuss. Thus, the cook-out combines the two surest forces for a lousy meal since the British discovered what boiling could do to beef.

Make no effort, therefore, to fly in the face of nature. Accept the facts that (1) the process of outdoor cooking will sear, scorch, and finally cremate whatever victim is sacrificed to it; and (2) you couldn't handle it if the situation were otherwise. Come up with a Specialty. Anything will do—barbecued frogs' legs, Mexican bean stew, curried shishkebab, meatless sukiyaki—anything! The worse the recipe, the less you have to apologize to yourself for. [Note: Whatever your dish, make certain that just before serving it you douse it liberally with a cheap domestic wine. This will convince all present they are about to partake of a "gourmet" dish.]

In setting up for the evening's festivities, two considerations should be borne in mind: (1) the hotter the fire, the quicker you'll be rid of the whole thing. Therefore, start that fire early in the afternoon and feed it unstintingly right up to the Cook's Moment. And (2) you want all the food, utensils, and culinary clutter imaginable at hand. All, that is, *except those items you will actually be needing*. It goes like this:

W.L.:   Well, about time to start those beef-liver burgers, I guess. Anybody hungry?

Intruder: Sounds good to me. Guess there isn't time for another drink?

W.L.:   Plenty of time. Way I cook them, these burgers really get *done*. Now let's see.... where'd I put that meat press? Christ, I forgot to bring it out. Oh, well, back to the ranch!

With a happy air of annoyance, W.L. trots off to The Kitchen. There, in privacy and comfort, he puts down a few Scotches while rummaging around in the utensil drawers.

The danger in all this lies in the Abuse of Privilege. *No host is permitted more than three forgets in one cook-out.* On the other hand, that's a helluva lot of good booze by any man's standards.

Later on, after your guests have finished eating what they can of whatever it was you cooked for them, serve a liqueur. (Yes, a *liqueur*!) Their greasy sweetness, their unmistakable kinship with cough medicine, and their outrageously *primary* colors make them practically impossible to drink. (Recommended: Creme de Violet.)

Your conduct during the remainder of the evening depends on both your imaginative powers and your need.

The Kitchen is there, close at hand, and (if you've played your cards right) untenanted. W.L. permits himself one phone call per cook-out. ("That was Lloyd. Wants me to help him with his out-rigger. But this time I made him get up a list of the things we'll be needing. He's always running back to the house for some damn thing he's forgotten.")

What with one thing and another, you should find no problem getting to The Kitchen four or five times during what's left of the evening. Then, warmed and comforted with the balm of booze, you exchange affectionate fare-wells with your guests, accept their murmured thanks, and sit down with your wife for a nightcap.

L'ENVOI

Late, quite late, W.L. is in a stupor. His wife, having finished the dishes and prepared herself for bed, enters the living room and circles his chair quietly, barefoot. She calls softly to him twice, to no avail. She kneels before him to unlace his shoes. Rising, she removes his necktie and opens his shirt. Just as she is gathering the remarkable strength in that small body to heft him to his feet and carry him off to bed, W.L. chuckles. From the depths of his coma, he says brightly, pleasantly, "Well, better luck next time."

And out of the truly lousy time her life has become, she smiles down at him. He is a good man, gentle and generous. However in God's earth he does it, he is a good provider. But things are too much for him; always have been. So he needs help and the help comes in bottles. . . .

If only, she sighs, hauling him to his feet, if only he could realize that he is an alcoholic. If he could say just once, even if only to himself, *I am an alcoholic.* Then we might make a start. Then we might get somewhere.